CEDAR RAPIDS

Our people, our story
Vol. 1

Published by

The Gazette

Printed by
Quebecor World

Cover Photo

STEPPING OUT
– The Shrine Parade through downtown Cedar Rapids was a big draw in the early 1920s. The marching unit is close to the corner of First Avenue and Third Street East. The YMCA can be seen in the background on the left. The photo was taken by William Baldridge, an early commercial photographer in Cedar Rapids. The U.S. Cellular Center is located in the block on the left today. By the time this parade picture was taken, Cedar Rapids was more than 70 years old. The first settlers had arrived in 1837 and 1838. There is some dispute as to who established the first claim: Osgood Shepherd or William Stone. But the first Linn County sheriff was Hosea W. Gray, appointed in 1838. More settlers arrived and the city grew with the organization of the first church, a Methodist, in 1843; the first school was erected in 1846-47; the post office established in 1847, and on Jan. 15, 1849, Cedar Rapids was incorporated by the Iowa Legislature. *(Submitted by Dan Sullivan)*

PREFACE

The changes in society and the community around us have never been more evident than when we peruse the hundreds of photographs in "Cedar Rapids: Our People, Our Story, Volume 1." These snapshots recorded every day life in the Cedar Rapids area during the relatively simpler times of the 1880s and 1890s and the first half of the 20th Century. Albeit two-dimensional, the black-and-white photographs are packed with information about people, where they worked, how they enjoyed life, and how they celebrated family milestones.

With the public's help, The Gazette is able to create an outstanding collection of rare and unusual local pictures made by amateur and professional photographers who captured moments in time and froze them in place. Responding to our call for old photographs, area residents submitted a wonderful variety of images, many of them pulled from aging albums or found in attic trunks and boxes in the basement. In addition, we were able to borrow historically relevant pictures from several local museums and, of course, we tapped The Gazette's extensive archive of news photographs.

The more than 300 photographs in this book are like pieces of tile in a mosaic. Collectively, they create a big, telling picture of the lives and times of people, places and activities of days gone by in the Cedar Rapids area.

By Mark Bowden
Gazette editor

Mark Bowden, Gazette editor, is shown working on a computer terminal in The Gazette newsroom in 1981. The Gazette has been in the building at the corner of Third Avenue and Fifth Street SE since 1925. (*Gazette photo*)

ACKNOWLEDGMENTS

CEDAR RAPIDS

Our people, our story

Vol. 1

THE PROJECT STAFF

Angie Kramer – Project Manager

Phyllis Fleming – Editor

Stacie Bedford – Marketing Manager

Pam Hyberger – Design and Layout

Joan Roberts – Clerical Assistant

Victoria Guyer – Production

Ed Faber, Mary Reeder – Media Consultants

Fran Roushar, Matt Thiessen, Terri Vosmek, Jill Hinke, Gregg Alliss – Photo Scanners

Terry Bergen – Consultant

GAZETTE ARCHIVE

John McGlothlen – Librarian

Diane Langton – Assistant Librarian

Roland Utsinger – Production Assistant

Paul Jensen – Director of Photography

THE HISTORY CENTER

Mark Hunter – Cedar Rapids historian

To all those who contributed to "CEDAR RAPIDS Our people, our story," we express our thanks and appreciation. Efforts were made to verify the information accompanying the photos by referring to Cedar Rapids city directories, Cedar Rapids and Linn County history books, Gazette archives, documents at The History Center and other area museums. However, names and other information on the back of photos and dates recalled by contributors might not have been exact. If you believe information is inaccurate or you have additional information, please send us the material so it can be sent to appropriate archives. Here's the address: Gazette Communications Marketing Department, 500 Third Ave. SE, PO Box 2525, Cedar Rapids, Iowa, 52406.

ANNIVERSARY PARADE

All decked out for the parade held in connection with the 50th anniversary of the Iowa Legislature's grant of a city charter to Cedar Rapids in 1906 are John Clarke, Henry Herman, Mary Harper, Anna Biederman, Barbara Raker, Tillie Janda, Anna Dudek, Nellie Cusack, Lena Krabenhofe, John Dysart and Harry Morgan. The women were employees of the Cedar Rapids Candy Co. and had previously worked at Quaker Oats. The town's first charter was adopted in 1849. The 1856 charter stood until April 6, 1908, when the city adopted the "commission plan." (*Submitted by Bill Biederman, nephew of Anna Biederman*)

TAILOR SHOP

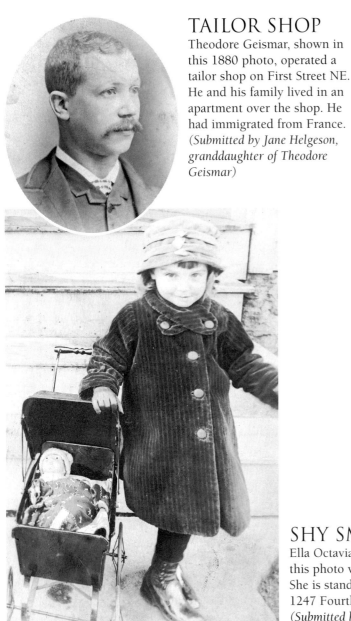

Theodore Geismar, shown in this 1880 photo, operated a tailor shop on First Street NE. He and his family lived in an apartment over the shop. He had immigrated from France. *(Submitted by Jane Helgeson, granddaughter of Theodore Geismar)*

SHY SMILE

Ella Octavia Cargin was 2 when this photo was taken in 1880. She is standing in front of 1247 Fourth St. SW. *(Submitted by Sheila Streight)*

SOLEMN GROUP

John and Helen Frish of 1818 S. Fourth St. are pictured with their children, John, Joe, Mary, Kate and Anna, in 1883. *(Submitted by Dorothy Nemecek)*

FAMILY PORTRAIT

The Frank M. Yost family is shown in Yost Hall in Center Point around 1888. In the back row are (from left) the Yosts' four children, Frank L. Yost, Jessie May Yost, B.B. Yost and Charles G. Yost. In the front row are (from left) Dr. Frank Yost and Charlotte Gitchell Yost. All three sons followed their father into the practice of medicine. Dr. Frank M. Yost was a doctor in Center Point from the mid-1800s to 1903. His son, Dr. Charles G. Yost, took over the practice that year and continued until his death in 1956. Dr. Charles Yost delivered more than 1,100 babies in the Center Point area. Dr. Kenneth Anderson, long-time doctor in Center Point, has had his residence in what was Yost Hall. *(Submitted by Ronald Lyman. Charles and Charity Ann Yost were his great-aunt and great-uncle)*

SCHOOL PICTURE

The fourth-grade class posed on the steps of what is believed to be Jefferson Elementary School at 716 A Ave. NE on May 3, 1890. Lillie Horsky, then 9, is one of the girls in the photo. She would have walked to the school from her home shown below.

FAMILY HOME

This narrow brick house at 119 Fifth St. NE was home to the Horsky family. Pictured in about 1893 are Catherine Barta Kimes (Grandma Kimes), Helen Horsky and four of her five daughters, Lill, Lib, Helen and Bess. Mrs. Kimes was Mrs. Horsky's mother. The house was located near what is now the Fifth Street NE entrance to the Five Seasons Parkade. *(Submitted by Carole Gauger, great-grand-daughter of Helen Horsky)*

BROTHERS
Charles, George and Arthur E. Johnson are shown in 1890. Their father died and they were raised by their mother, Mary Jane, in Toddville. (*Submitted by Louise Johnson*)

SHOW TIME – This elegantly dressed crowd fills the four tiers of seats at Greene's Opera House in about 1890. Built in 1880, Greene's booked the best Broadway shows on tour and other touring companies. There would be entertainment nearly every night. After leaving Chicago, the road companies played Cedar Rapids, Omaha and Denver, en route to San Francisco. Carriages would be lined up for blocks as patrons of the theater stepped to the high board sidewalk on North Second Street, across the street from The Roosevelt. A 1958 Gazette story about the opera house says the stage was large enough to accommodate the chariot race in "Ben Hur," with teams of horses galloping on a rotating tread. The upper balconies were not reserved and teenagers would line up for hours before the box office opened in order to get front-row seats. Later, the Majestic theater, which booked the country's top vaudeville acts plus stage shows, cut into Greene's business and the opening of movie theaters from 1915 into the 1920s spelled the end for the opera house. (*Submitted by John McIvor*)

A pioneering spirit for more than 150 years.

The Next Stage®

In 1852, Henry Wells and William G. Fargo founded a company that became a legendary part of the American West. For over 150 years, the Wells Fargo name has been synonymous with outstanding customer service and reliable delivery.

From offices throughout California's gold country, trustworthy Wells Fargo agents provided essential banking services, reliable transportation of gold and goods, and dependable mail delivery to frontier miners, merchants, and settlers. Wells Fargo transported treasure, mail, and express shipments by the fastest means available: stagecoach, steamship or Pony Express. Viewed as a lifeline to civilized society, the Wells Fargo coach meant the arrival of old friends, letters from loved ones and important packages. Wells Fargo agents set up shop at stations along the stage routes and then followed railroad workers building tracks across the West. In November, 1866, Wells Fargo took control of the major western stage lines. After a golden spike completed the transcontinental railroad in May of 1869, Wells Fargo's fortunes rode the rails.

Iowa was criss-crossed by the stages of the Western Stage Company, wherever there weren't railroad lines, including into Cedar Rapids into the 1860s. At that time, Wells Fargo offices extended only as far east as Omaha. From there, any deliveries for Iowa were ferried across the Missouri River to Council Bluffs and transferred to Iowa express lines.

Wells Fargo & Co, Express opened in Cedar Rapids in 1909, at the Chicago, Milwaukee and St. Paul railroad depot. Albert Hotchkins served as the first agent in Cedar Rapids. The current bank building at 101 3rd Avenue was originally built for People's Savings Bank, which later became Wells Fargo through merger. It was designed by famed architect Louis Sullivan in 1910.

Wells Fargo has a long history of blazing new trails to take our customers where they want to go — from stagecoach routes to the information highway to the financial services of tomorrow. Your dreams are the first stage. Wells Fargo. *The Next Stage.*

FLORIST CREW

These men are working in Kramer & Son floral shop on Third Avenue in about 1890. Early city directories showed addresses in both the 200 and 300 block of Third Avenue SE. Owners were Isaac and Judson Kramer. Shop did both wholesale and retail business. Photo was taken by William Baylis, a professional photographer who took many early Cedar Rapids photos.
(Submitted by Bill Kuba)

GAZETTE IN 1890S

From 1888 to 1925, The Gazette was in this building on First Avenue on the east bank of the Cedar River near the bridge. The next move was to the building now occupied at Third Avenue and Fifth Street SE.
(Gazette photo)

Celebrating
150 years

Tradition

Shuttleworth & Ingersoll P.L.C. traces its roots back to 1854 when Nathaniel Hubbard opened a law practice in Marion. When the firm moved to Cedar Rapids in 1870 Hubbard had added three partners to become "Hubbard, Dawley, Grimm & Wheeler." As new partners entered the firm, its name changed several times until becoming "Shuttleworth & Ingersoll" in 1962.

Client Service and Community Involvement

Shuttleworth & Ingersoll has earned and maintained a widespread reputation for high quality legal work and exceptional client service. Shuttleworth & Ingersoll lawyers are proud of their involvement in community and civic affairs. Three Iowa Supreme Court Justices have come from the ranks of the firm over years, and dozens of Shuttleworth & Ingersoll lawyers have held and continue to hold important leadership positions in local, state and national professional and nonprofit organizations.

The Firm owes its success and longevity to its clientele and its attorneys and staff who have served them well for many years. Shuttleworth & Ingersoll cherishes its history and looks forward to a promising future.

T. M. "Ty" Ingersoll

V.C. "Craven"
Shuttleworth

SHUTTLEWORTH & INGERSOLL, P.L.C.
ATTORNEYS AT LAW   ESTABLISHED 1854

115 THIRD STREET SE CEDAR RAPIDS, IOWA
TELEPHONE 319.365.9461   FACSIMILE 319.365.8725   WWW.SHUTTLEWORTHLAW.COM

MOTHER AND SON

Clara Melinda Nelson Stephenson Muehlenberg of Cedar Rapids is shown with her 3-year-old son, Walter Rae Stephenson, in this 1894 photo. *(Submitted by Betty Mineck)*

RIDING THE RAILS

This Cedar Rapids railroad handcart crew is pictured in 1890. Seven of the men are identified as follows: Cleve Bennett, George Mann, Floyd Scholley, George Bruce, Charles Stroff (third from right), Gus Johnson and Charles Roher, *(Submitted by William Neff)*

MILLIGAN FAMILY

Members of the Milligan family stand in front of their Linn County home in about 1895. They are (from left) John Sherman Milligan, Amanda Reeves Milligan, William H. Milligan and Myra Jane Churchill Milligan. In 1916, a new house was built at a cost of $3,000 just to the west of this one. That house still stands today at 5757 Kirkwood Blvd. SW. *(Submitted by Don Milligan)*

NEIGHBORHOOD STORE

There were dozens of neighborhood grocery stores in early Cedar Rapids. In 1896 P. Mineck Groceries and Meats was at 821 Third Ave. SW. Peter Mineck bought the grocery store, goods and land for $250.

As the 1932 picture (below) shows the store grew over the years and continued to be operated by the family. Gus Mineck managed the grocery department and his brother, Arnold Peter Mineck, managed the meat department. Arnold Mineck is at left in this photo; Gus Mineck is in the center of the group of three men. The store, always at the same location, operated until the early 1950s. *(Submitted by Betty Mineck)*

WEDDING DAY

Eva Antonia Chulupsky and Fred Langhurst are pictured on their wedding day in Cedar Rapids in 1898. She was 18. Fred Langhurst, who worked as a carpenter, had immigrated from Germany when he was 17. *(Submitted by Carly Langhurst, great-granddaughter of the Langhursts)*

PART OF CEDAR RAPIDS

SINCE 1873

"Finally *(Robert Stuart, Quaker Oats co-founder)* saw what he wanted: the most magnificent quality oats in the world in abundant supply. They were grown in the eight-foot deep topsoil of Eastern Iowa...

Nobody had ever seen such oats, and Cedar Rapids on the swift flowing Cedar River there was a likely and available site for a mill."

*EXCERPT FROM BRANDS
TRADEMARKS AND GOODWILL*

*THE STORY OF THE QUAKER
OATS COMPANY*

QUAKER

418 2 ST NE • CEDAR RAPIDS • IOWA

WOMEN'S RELIEF CORPS

Members of the WRC from Central City and Prairieburg posed for this photo on May 30, 1898. Front row (left to right): Lydia A. Drexler, Mrs. Shakespeare, Mrs. Caryl (Ike's mother), Mrs. Simeon Blodgett (Joe's mother), Mrs. Butters, Mrs. Walker (Carrie Brunen's mother), Mrs. Shaffer (photographer's wife), Mrs. Abaile Brown (Cara Edgerley's mother), Mrs. Mills (A.D.'s mother: Second row: Mrs. Pipes (Wib's mother), Mrs. Burns, Mrs. Giffen (Adelia), Mrs. Austin Blodgett (Myrta Cunningham's mother), Mrs. Trueblood, Mrs. H.G. Porter, Mrs. G.D. (Dane) Gillilan (Floy Knapton's mother), Mrs. Perry Cook, Mrs. Reid (Abbie Epperson's mother). The names were listed as they were printed in the newspaper. There was no explanation why the names in parenthesis were listed. (*Submitted by Kathy Carnahan, great-granddaughter of Mrs. Perry Cook*)

B STREET BAR

The bar owned by Jan and Antonio Stastny was located at the southeast corner of B Street and 17th Avenue SW in 1898. Patrons leaned on the wooden bar as they were served. (*Submitted by Bill Kuba*)

Jacketed Cream Can ▲

JG Cherry invented and patented the Cherry Jacketed Cream Can with which he founded his business in 1880. The original can was composed of a circular tin inner lining and outer wooden jacket.

Air space between the layers served as insulation and a unique interior float helped prevent churning during the wagon trip over rough roads.

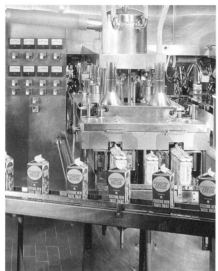

▲ Half-gallon and quart gable top carton fillers

Introduced in 1966, a line of stainless steel packaging machines used to form, fill and seal gable top cartons marked a turning point in dairy plant technology. The line continues to be manufactured in Cedar Rapids.

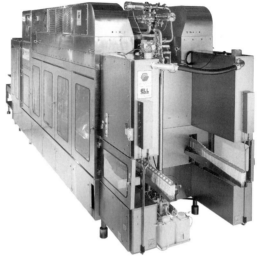

◀ Gable top carton filler

Extended Long LIfe machines represent state-of-the-art sanitary packaging design, combining several proven technologies to help packagers protect products from potential contamination. Today's models include much more sophisticated technology.

▲BFAH-30 Bottle Filler

The most recent diversification into bottle filling machines offers high-quality, versatile, efficient and economical bottling solutions.

▼Cherry Building 329 10th Ave SE, circa 1912

▲ Logos over the years

JG Cherry Co., established in 1880, merged with DH Burrell of Little Falls, NY in 1928, forming the Cherry-Burrell Company.

▲ Present location 2400 6th St. SW

PICKLE WORKS

The Star Pickle Works was at 113 First St. SW in about 1899. Products were pickles, vinegar, mustard and pickled meats. *(Submitted by Bill Kuba)*

READY FOR RESIDENTS

The Home for Aged Women at the corner of 12th Street and A Avenue NW was new when this photo was taken in 1899. The yard is still being worked on. Today known as Kingston Hill, the facility is providing both women and men with a home. *(Submitted by Vivian Rinaberger)*

FIREFIGHTERS

This crew worked at Cedar Rapids Hose House No. 4 at 1111 Third St. SE, next to the CSPS Hall, around 1900. *(Submitted by Bill Kuba)*

WHEELS APLENTY

Bicycles were a popular form of transportation in 1900 when this picture was taken at the Stepanek and Vondracek Hardware Store at 201-203 Second Ave. SE. William Akers works on a bike in the foreground. One of the owners, W.H. Stepanek, is shown in the oval photo. *(Submitted by Kathy Hartgrave, granddaughter of William Akers)*

U.R. NEXT

That's what the sign on the window of this barber shop at the corner of 12th Avenue and Sixth Street SE said in the early 1900s. *(Submitted by Vivian Rinaberger)*

The power to help a community grow

L ike many Midwest towns, circuses were responsible for bringing the first electric lights to Cedar Rapids. When the W.C. Coup Circus came to town in May 1882, people lined up to see the marvelous new "arc light" on display. Soon after, on August 18, 1882 the Cedar Rapids Electric Light and Power Company was founded by a group of prominent businessmen.

In 1903, the company formed the Cedar Rapids and Iowa City Railroad (CRANDIC) and changed its name to Iowa Railway and Light Company. Over the years, the company expanded and in 1932 changed its name to Iowa Electric Light and Power Company. (IE).

By the 1930s electricity delivery improved so much that by 1938 more than a third of American homes had a refrigerator. The electrification of office equipment soon became standard nationwide.

A study carried out by IE indicated a need to help women learn the value of electricity in the American home. As a result, the utility developed the Home Services Department, and one of its projects was a model electrified home known as the "Bungalow." From the Cedar

Rapids headquarters, weekly *Bungalow Notes* provided advice about home lighting, interior decorating, food talks, menus, recipes, diet programs and the history of various foods.

The company marked another milestone when the Atomic Energy Commission issued an operating license for Iowa's first nuclear power station in 1974. In June of that year commercial operation began at the Duane Arnold Energy Center, which remains Iowa's only nuclear plant.

In 1998, IES Industries, Interstate Power Co., and Wisconsin Power & Light, completed the nation's first three-way utility merger to form Alliant Energy.

Today Alliant Energy continues to grow and expand in its role in bringing safe, reliable energy to Cedar Rapids and more than one million customers throughout the Midwest.

ALLIANT ENERGY

We're on for you.

IN STEP

Members of the Mentzer Drill Team step out at the Linn County fairgrounds in Marion about 1900. The Indian Creek Country Club is at this location today. (*Submitted by Vivian Rinaberger*)

READY TO RIDE

Moyer & Darling Bicycles was at 110 Second St. NE in 1900. Earl Darling, part owner of the store, stands in the middle. Note the wooden sidewalks. (*Submitted by Frances Green, daughter of Earl Darling*)

HIGH STEPPERS

Trotting races were popular at county fairs in the early 1900s. This scene was at the Linn County Fair in Marion. (*Submitted by F&M Bank*)

READY TO SERVE

A restaurant owned by Marshall Perkins was in operation on Second Street SE in the late 1890s. In this picture from about 1900, the staff stands on the front steps. Perkins was the first African-American member of the Cedar Rapids Chamber of Commerce. The restaurant was in a block of other businesses operated by African-Americans. (*African American Historical Museum and Cultural Center of Iowa photo*)

Bill Baylis used a photo of himself to promote his photo business in Cedar Rapids, probably in the 1920s. (*Submitted by Bill Kuba*)

PICNIC AT PALISADES

This group of young people from Cedar Rapids are shown at Palisades Park in Linn County in the early 1900s. Bill Baylis, a professional photographer in early Cedar Rapids, is at far right using one of his favorite tricks. The hat over his hand covers the string that he was using to trigger the camera. This allowed him to get in the picture with his friends. Baylis is credited with taking an estimated 25,000 photos. Many of them are in the collection of The History Center. (*History Center photo*)

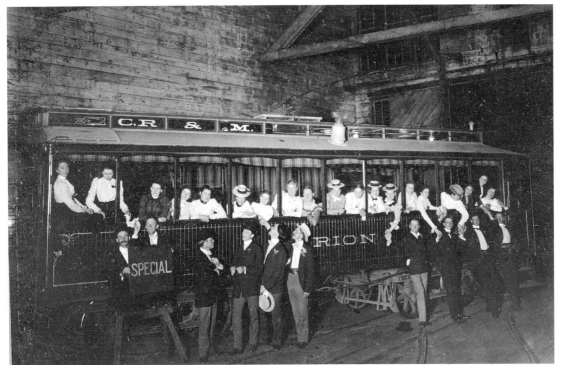

PARTY TIME

This group of young people is partying in the trolley barn at Second Street NE in the early 1900s. The initials on the car stand for Cedar Rapids and Marion. Streetcar service between Cedar Rapids and Marion started in 1880. The cars were initially powered by steam; the system was electrified in 1890. *(Submitted by Vivian Rinaberger)*

HERE'S LOOKING AT YOU

Maynard W. Rowray and his team of goats are shown at the corner of Second Avenue and First Street SE about 1904. The building on the left was taken down to make way for the federal courthouse in 1931-32. *(Submitted by Jack Rowray, son of Maynard Rowray.)*

SUITED UP

George Neff played football in college in 1900. Originally from Omaha, he later taught school in Viola and then worked as a streetcar conductor in Cedar Rapids and Marion. *(Submitted by William Neff, son of George Neff)*

BANKING BUSINESS

This is believed to be the office for the Iowa State Savings Bank in the early 1900s. Early city directories showed two addresses for the bank, both on Third Street SE. One of those addresses, 1201 Third St. SE, is where Village Bank and Trust is today. (*Submitted by F&M Bank*)

BUSY DEPOT

This was the scene in the early 1900s on the track side of the Union Depot between Third and Fourth avenues SE. Greene Square is in the foreground. The park was named for Judge George Greene, active in the early development of Cedar Rapids as a city. (*Submitted by F&M Bank*)

Keeping pace with the health-care demands of a growing community.

For more than 100 years, Mercy Medical Center has been the place where **the Mercy Touch** comes to life. It is the extra measure of genuine compassion and understanding that we provide. It is our staff of skilled professionals working with the latest advances in medical technology. It is the many ways we improve life in our community.

701 10th Street SE, Cedar Rapids, IA • www.mercycare.org

IN TUNE

Members of the girls' chorus gather on the steps of Washington High School in the early 1900s. Director Alice Inskeep is in the center of the back row. Helen Kacena is second from left in the top row. Johannah Hahn is at the right end of the front row. Washington was on Fourth Avenue SE across from Greene Square. Cedar Rapids started naming schools for presidents in 1875. *(Submitted by JoAnne Havran, daughter of Johannah Hahn)*

KENWOOD PARK

The town of Kenwood Park, incorporated in 1886, was between Cedar Rapids and Marion. Barnet Lutz was the town's first mayor. The town was on the trolley line between the two cities. Kenwood became part of Cedar Rapids in 1927. The location of the New Store is where the Irish Democrat and other businesses are today near the corner of First Avenue and 32nd Street SE. *(Submitted by F&M Bank)*

SUNDAY STROLL – This was the scene in Bever Park on a sunny afternoon in the early 1900s. The land was donated to the city in 1900 for use as a park by James L. Bever Jr. as a memorial to his grandfather, Sampson Bever, a banker who had settled in Cedar Rapids in 1851. At the time, the park was described as being in the woods to the east of the city. (*Submitted by F&M Bank*)

THREE FRIENDS

This photo, taken in Cedar Rapids in 1902, was titled *"A Day in Autumn."* The women are cousins Alice Darragh and Alice Roddy (now Mrs. G. Hannon) and Irma Biederman. *(Submitted by Bill Biederman, son of Irma Biederman)*

BETTER BUTTER

The sign on the side of the Blue Valley Creamery wagon at left promotes butter and says that it is churned fresh every day. The creamery was at 400 Ninth Ave. SE in the early 1900s. *(Submitted by Vivian Rinaberger)*

RIDING IN STYLE

Gazette publisher Clarence Miller (right) was owner of the first gasoline-powered car in Cedar Rapids in 1901. Fire Chief Fred Cook and Gazette Editor Fred Faulkes are in the buggy. Miller was an early fan of the automobile; Faulkes, on the other hand, always preferred a horse and buggy and often would refuse to ride in a car. Photo was taken on the A Avenue viaduct. *(Gazette photo)*

READY
TO RIDE

Wesley Suchomel
is ready to ride
in this 1903
photo in
Cedar Rapids.
(*Submitted by
Dorothy Nemecek*)

CARNIVAL WEEK

The young women of Cedar Lodge No. 1 of the Iowa Legion of Honor are ready to participate in a Carnival Week parade in Cedar Rapids in the early 1900s. Carnival Week was held in October for several years. *"Tales of the Town"* by Ralph Clements said that a different parade was held each day. First Presbyterian Church, 310 Fifth St. SE, is at left in background.

ON THE STUMP

Orator William Jennings Bryan is shown campaigning in Cedar Rapids in the 1900s. The train was stopped at Union Station and Greene Square is to the right. Nationally known as an orator and political speaker, he was a perennial attraction on the Chautauqua circuit developed by Keith Vawter of Cedar Rapids in 1904. Other favorites were Edgar Bergen, James Whitcomb Riley and the Sousa band. Bryan, a Democrat, was candidate for president three times. He first ran in 1896. During one campaign he made more than 600 speeches in 27 states. He also appeared at the 1902 Carnival Week parade in Cedar Rapids shown at right. (*Photos submitted by Bill Kuba*)

FRINK FAMILY
– All but two members of the Orvin Frink family are in this 1904 photo. Standing are daughters Blanche (Johnson), Nellie (Slocum) and Mattie (Wentworth). Seated are the father of the family, Orvin Kent Frink, and sons Prentice, Orvin Jr., Bert and Roland. The family lived in Lisbon. (*Submitted by Louise Johnson*)

BIG PROJECT
The arrow points to ironworker Dana L. Stearns, who was part of the crew building the Bosch-Ryan Elevator about 1903. The elevator was east of the Iowa Railway and Light Co. Power House on Sixth Street NE. Stearns also was an amateur photographer and took many photos in the 1890s. (*Submitted by Larry Beatty*)

CLASS PICTURE
Dressed in their best for a class picture are first graders at Madison School at Second Avenue and Third Street SW in 1903. Mrs. Ramsdal was the teacher. Today's Madison school is at 1341 Woodside Dr. NW. (*Submitted by Jean Doran*)

FIRST CRANDIC CAR

Avondale streetcar No. 1 was CRANDIC's first passenger car. Conductor Wilson C. Stookey and motorman Harry Price are shown here on June 4, 1904. The CRANDIC officially began service as an interurban electric railroad on Aug. 13, 1904. Construction on tracks for the Cedar Rapids and Iowa City Railway began in 1903. A line to Mount Vernon was completed in 1913 and went on to Lisbon in 1914. That service ended in 1928. There were 60 passenger stops between Cedar Rapids and Iowa City. (*CRANDIC photo*)

RAIL SPLITTERS

This semi-pro team played its home games at a field near the Wilson Packing House by Sinclair Park in southeast Cedar Rapids. The team also traveled within a 50-mile radius of Cedar Rapids, including towns such as Cascade and Monticello. Bill Biederman is at top left. (*Submitted by Bill Biederman, son of Bill Biederman*)

DRESSED FOR WORK

Charles Hadish Sr. (center) and co-workers are pictured in the CRANDIC freight office in Iowa City in the early 1900s. (*Submitted by Louise Hadish*)

TICK TOCK

Joseph Moll stands in his jewelry store, which was at the corner of First Street and Second Avenue SE in 1904. He and his wife lived in an apartment above the store.

Vernona Moll, 17, is shown at work in Moll's Jewelry Store at First Street and Second Avenue SE. She was the daughter of the owner, Joseph Moll. *(Both submitted by Jeanne Jontz, Vernona's granddaughter)*

STILL STANDING

Mary Bousek and an unidentified child stand outside Mary's house at 92 19th Ave. SW about 1904. Her daughter and son-in-law, Emma and Mike Gallagher, live there today. *(Submitted by John Gallagher)*

SCHOOL LUNCH

Harrison school teachers and Assistant Principal Louis Ling (right) gathered for lunch in the school's kindergarten room in 1904. Mabel Alice Real McLaughlin (far left) taught fifth grade at Harrison, which was at the corner of Sixth Street and K Avenue NW. *(Submitted by Frances Stauffacher, daughter of Mrs. McLaughlin)*

GROUNDBREAKING

Westminster Presbyterian Church got a new name and a new location in 1904 and 1905 respectively. The first church built in 1858 was at the corner of Third Avenue and Third Street SE. It was known as the Presbyterian Church of Cedar Rapids. In 1868-69, the name was changed to Second Presbyterian. The church was expanded in 1872. Then on April 30, 1904, ground was broken at the corner in Wellington Heights where Bever Avenue, Third Avenue and 14th Street SE come together. The new church was renamed Westminster Presbyterian and dedicated in May 1905. As this photo shows, there was a good turnout for the groundbreaking. *(Submitted by Westminster Presbyterian Church)*

QUAKER CREW

Employees are shown outside the Quaker Oats mill in Cedar Rapids in about 1905. The original North Star Oatmeal Mill opened in 1873. In 1891, North Star was merged into a conglomerate of 20-some cereal plants known as the American Cereal Co. That became Quaker Oats in 1901. (*Submitted by Bill Biederman*)

IOWA STEEL CREW

In the early 1900s when this photo was taken, Iowa Steel and Iron Works and the J.G. Cherry Co. were close to each other and this group may include men from both plants. They became friends and shared many activities. Iowa Steel was at 400-412 12th Ave. SE and Cherry was at the corner of Tenth Avenue and Fourth Street SE. (*Submitted by Bill Biederman*)

CHERRY EMPLOYEES

A group of J.G. Cherry employees stands in front of the plant at the corner of 10th Avenue and Fourth Street SE around 1905. The refurbished Cherry Building, 329 10th Ave. SE, was a former Cherry warehouse built in 1919. In 1948, the plant, then known as Cherry-Burrell, was moved to the current site at 2400 Sixth St. SW. Today, it's known as Evergreen Packaging Equipment. In 1928, Cherry merged with the Burrell dairy equipment plant and five other dairy-related businesses to become Cherry-Burrell. The first Cherry product, a wooden and tin cream can that insulated cream from extreme hot or cold temperatures, was invented by J.G. Cherry. (*Submitted by Bill Biederman*)

COOL DELIVERY

Henry Fix (left) was part of a three-man crew from Hubbard's Ice at 1124 First St. NW in 1905. They delivered blocks of ice for home ice boxes. Note the tongs over each man's left or right shoulder. (*Submitted by John McIvor, grandson of Henry Fix.*)

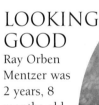

LOOKING GOOD

Ray Orben Mentzer was 2 years, 8 months old when he smiled for the camera in 1906 in Cedar Rapids. (*Submitted by Sheila Streight*)

SITTING FOR PORTRAIT

A woman believed to be Leliah Warren of Cedar Rapids and an unidentified child sit for their portrait in about 1905. *(African American Historical Museum and Cultural Center of Iowa photo)*

FILL 'ER UP

This crew at Cedar Rapids Bottling Co. included Ned Ford in the foreground in 1905. The plant was located at 118 First St. NW. The brand name was Hur-Mon. *(Submitted by Bill Kuba)*

WORKING WOMEN

This room full of seamstresses worked for the Perfection Mfg. Company at 403 Second Ave. SE in the early 1900s. This later was converted to the Lincoln/Taft Hotel. *(Submitted by Vivian Rinaberger)*

CELEBRATION

In 1906, Cedar Rapids had a big celebration noting the 50th anniversary of the charter granted the city by the Iowa Legislature. These young women are in Riverside Park between Ninth and 14th avenues SW. Four of them are identified as follows: Mary Sojka, Anna Sleger, Olga Kolarik and Stella Anderson. (*Submitted by Jane Aldrich, granddaughter of Olga Kolarik*)

SEE DER RABBITS

In the early years, the name of Cedar Rapids was sometimes converted to See Der Rabbits as a joke. That theme was carried out in this parade. If you look closely at this 1906 photo, you will find many rabbits. Check the awning of the Armstrong and McGlenahan clothing store on the right and on the left the Denecke and Yetter sign. And there's a big rabbit in the crowd in the foreground. The parade is moving along Second Street between First and Second avenues SE. (*Submitted by Bill Kuba*)

ALAMO PARK – The amusement park opened in 1906 on 11th Street NW near where Roosevelt Middle School is today. The park, pictured here on June 9, 1906, featured a figure-eight roller coaster 50 feet high and 1,550 feet long, "Mentzer's Electric Shoot-the-Chutes," and a 100-foot-tall Ferris wheel. (*Submitted by Sheila Streight*)

SERIOUS BUSINESS

These solemn-looking people were members of the mid-winter class in January 1906 of the Iowa Consistory, Scottish Rite Masons. The Masonic Temple was at First Street and First Avenue NE, a building that also housed the headquarters of the Order of Railway Conductors. Calvin Greene was Venerable Master of the first Scottish Rite lodge in 1884. (*Submitted by Cedar Rapids Scottish Rite Masons*)

SERVING RAIL PASSENGERS

The Clifton Hotel at First Avenue and Fourth Street SE was one of several hotels located along the tracks that served travelers arriving by train. The hotel was destroyed in 1903 by a fire in which 11 guests died. It was replaced by the Allison Hotel, which was the first modern fireproof hotel in Cedar Rapids. (*Submitted by Vivian Rinaberger*)

DECKED OUT FOR A RIDE

Dressed in what appear to be the latest styles are Helen Horsky, Bess Sullivan, Lillian Novotny and Alta Heil. The men are Steve Novotny and Bill Heil. Photo was taken in Cedar Rapids in 1907. They are standing in the 100 block of Fifth Street NE. *(Submitted by Carole Gauger)*

DOWNTOWN

The corner of Third Street and Second Avenue SE has long been a business focus. When this photo was taken in the early 1900s, M.M. Thompson Hatters and Haberdashers was on the first floor and various offices were on the second. It was known as the Kimball Building. Earlier this site was the location of the Blair Building that housed a number of the companies involved in the early railroads in Cedar Rapids. It was built in 1869 by John Blair of Blairstown, N.J., active in westward railroad construction. In 1925 the site was cleared to make way for the 12-story Merchants National Bank, now U.S. Bank. *(Submitted by Dr. D.A. Paulsen)*

PICTURE TIME

Members of the Greene's Opera House baseball club are shown on June 6, 1909. It is believed the photo was taken across from the opera house, which was located on Second Street NE between First and A avenues. Built in 1880, it seated 1,800. The billboard in the background refers to Alamo Park, a large amusement park located in the area where Roosevelt Middle School is today. The photo was taken by William Baylis and is owned by The History Center. Baylis has been credited with taking 25,000 photos of people and places in early Cedar Rapids. (*History Center photo*)

CANDY MAN

Clyde Satterly Sr. delivers candy for the Cedar Rapids Candy Co. in 1909, using his own team of horses. Later his son, Chester, would deliver for the same company but do it by car. *(Submitted by Cheryl Schatzle)*

HIKE

The Cedar Rapids High School football team is shown practicing in about 1909. At the time there was just one high school, Washington, located on Fourth Avenue SE across from Greene Square. *(Submitted by Robert Rowell)*

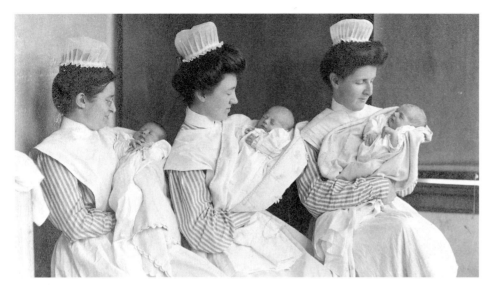

ROCK-A-BYE-BABY

Blanche Frink graduated from the St. Luke's Hospital registered nurse program in 1909 and then went to work at St. Luke's. This photo was taken from her "My Memory Book." On the first page, she recalls "a happy time where I first met a boy who I much later married." Here she is shown with two other nurses. From left: Laura Bradley, Edna Knight (Watters) and Blanche Frink (Johnson). (*Submitted by Louise Johnson*)

FAMILY OUTING

This photo was taken about 1909 by William Baylis, early Cedar Rapids photographer, probably in the Wellington Heights area of Cedar Rapids. Wellington Heights was named for Wellington Higley, one of four brothers active in many business ventures in early Cedar Rapids. The other brothers were Henry, Harvey and Mortimer. The photo is one of many Baylis photos given to The History Center. The family probably posed in front of their home. (*History Center photo*)

DELIVERY DAY – Drivers for the delivery trucks for Whelihan's Drug Store at 217 Third St. SE appear to be ready to spring into action in about 1910. (*Submitted by F&M Bank*)

NEIGHBORHOOD STORE

The Sterling Grocery, operated by Joe and Blanche Zisko, was in this building in 1914. It was on F Avenue NW, a block from where Norwood Promotional Products, formerly Souvenir Pencil, is today at 202 F Ave. NW. A dairy and a bakery were across the street. *(Submitted by George Oujiri, nephew of the Ziskos)*

CLEAN SWEEP

The crew of Troy Laundry at 214 First St. SW got their picture taken in about 1910. *(Submitted by F&M Bank)*

HEADED FOR MARION

George Frederick Neff was conductor and Mr. Franklin the motorman on the streetcar that ran to Marion and back in about 1910. Note the sign promoting Chautaqua in the window. For one week every summer, residents could attend afternoon and evening programs held in a large tent on the old athletic field at Coe College. Topics ranged from entertainment to religious inspiration. The idea was developed in 1904 by Keith Vawter of Cedar Rapids. Speakers and performers traveled a circuit that covered middle-sized cities around the country for some three decades. Union Station is in the background. (*Submitted by William Neff*)

STREET SCENE –
The intersection in the background is C Street and 16th Avenue SW in 1910. Although one car can be seen on the left, most people were traveling in horse-drawn wagons or on bicycles. Trolley tracks run down the middle of the dirt street. Bridge over the Cedar River can be seen in the background. Building on far left is today's Czech Cottage. (*Submitted by Debra Hawes*)

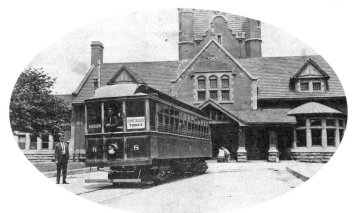

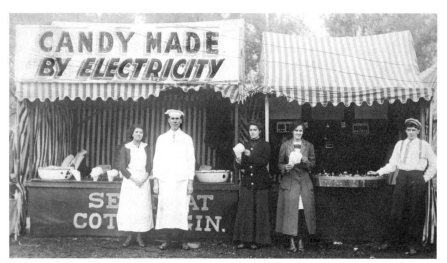

COTTON CANDY

Bess Horsky (second from right) was ready to sample the cotton candy during the Cedar Rapids Exposition held from Oct. 2 to 7 in 1911. The candy makers worked in the tents. The location may have been 13th Street NW near where Roosevelt Middle School is today. (*Submitted by Carole Gauger*)

SCHOOL PICTURE

Dressed in their best for a school picture are boys and girls in the fifth grade at Polk School at 1500 B Ave. NE in 1911. Many of the boys wear ties and the girls have large hair bows. *(Submitted by Vivian Rinaberger)*

HEADING HOME

Harold and Fern Cushman were ready for a ride. They were the children of Catherine and Ralph Cushman and lived on L Street SW. The photo was used on a postcard in 1913. *(Submitted by William Dale)*

LET'S PUT ON A PLAY

Miss Diehl's students from Trinity Methodist Church, 408 Third Ave. SW, were all in costume for a play when this was taken Feb. 21, 1912. Despite the suits and hats, all are women. The only person identified is Hazel Mentzer Cargin, who is fifth from left in the back row. She was a member of Trinity. (*Submitted by Sheila Streight, granddaughter of Hazel Cargin*)

TRINITY
MISS DIEHL'S CLASS 2 – 21 – '12

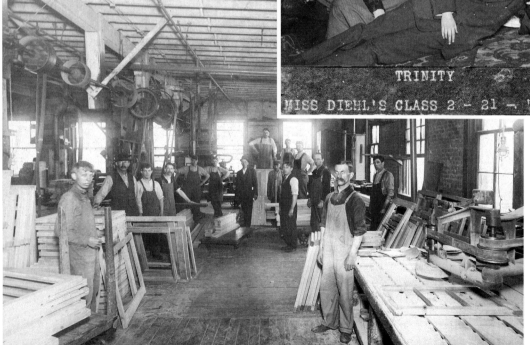

BUILT TO LAST

It was June 1912 when the work crew of Williams & Hunting, a door and sill company at 445 First St. SW, posed in the shop. Brothers Ed and John Vlasek were among the employees. (*Submitted by Anna Mae Vlasek*)

READY FOR MESSAGE

The choir came from five churches, Trinity, First United Brethren, Evangelical, Olivet and Reformed, for the West Side Union Service on Jan. 15, 1912. The evangelist, the Rev. Mr. Mahood, is seated at the left end of the front row. The choir leader, Mr. George, is standing in the middle of the front row. Mrs. George and Miss Mentzer, the organist, are at upper left. *(Submitted by Sheila Streight)*

CITY VIEW

This photo used on a postcard shows First Avenue West looking northeast in about 1910. The photographer was standing on 12th Street and First Avenue West. *(Submitted by Verla Mullins)*

ICE HARVEST

A crew from Hubbard's Ice at 1124 First St. NW cuts blocks of ice in the Cedar River. This photo was taken about 1925 from the Northwestern Railroad bridge. Each block weighed about 300 pounds and, once it was harvested, went into storage in an ice house near the river. Usually by August, most of the ice had been purchased and sometimes ice had to be brought in from further north by train. There was no mechanical refrigeration at this time and most households had ice boxes to keep food cool. Although the Hubbard name was used, the company was owned by the Chadima family. (*Submitted by Bill Kuba*)

ICY ASSEMBLY LINE

This loading operation was at Chadima Brothers Ice at First Street and L Avenue NW in the early 1900s. The blocks of ice each weighing about 300 pounds were being harvested from the nearby Cedar River. Each one went through a mechanical scrapper before going up the electrified conveyor belt. The blocks went into the wooden ice house in the background. When this picture was taken, the building was almost full because the blocks are going up the top conveyor belt. Sawdust was used to insulate the walls and each layer of ice was covered with straw or hay. The ice harvest was usually completed by the middle of February and the ice could be stored through the summer unless it was extremely hot, according to Bob Chadima. But he said usually they were out of ice by the end of August. In the early years there were two ice companies, Hubbard, owned by Charles Hubbard, and Chadima, owned by brothers Joe and Tom. The two companies merged in 1922. Then, in 1929, Chadima bought Hubbard but continued to use the Hubband name. An accompanying picture shows the blocks of ice being harvested from the river in about 1925. (*Submitted by F&M Bank*)

SERVED TRAIN PASSENGERS

The Second Ave. Virginia opened in 1914 at 329 Second Ave. SE. Owners John and Paul Costas and their staff served many railroad passengers when trains were stopped on the nearby tracks and people would get off looking for a place to eat. The restaurant was open 24 hours a day. Paul Costas stands at right; John is in the middle in the back. They operated this restaurant into the late 1920s and then in 1932 opened the Harmony Cafeteria at 118 Third St. SE. The Harmony was in operation until 1961 when it was purchased to make way for the Merchants National Bank parking lot and drive-in bank. The windows at the left are still in the building. Later, the Dragon was in this same location for many years. (*Submitted by Mike Costas, son of John Costas and nephew of Paul Costas*)

READY FOR RIDE

Robert and Blanche Rice of 110 14th St. SE, are shown with other family members just before leaving on a Sunday drive in 1913. (*Submitted by Jane Helgeson, daughter of Robert and Blanche Rice*)

TIME OUT

Floyd Turkal of Cedar Rapids is part of this group called the Rock Island Rough Riders, pictured in Decorah in 1913. Turkal was a Rock Island engineer. (*Submitted by Janice Hunter*)

THE ROCK ISLAND ROUGH RIDERS AT DECORAH, IA. 6-29-1913

HATS OFF

The work crew at the Cedar Rapids Carriage Works apparently liked variety in their hat styles. The plant was located at the corner of Second Street and 12th Avenue SE. The men built business wagons and did carriage and automobile repairing and painting. The photo was taken April 29, 1913. (*Submitted by Bill Kuba*)

MOVING DAY

Joseph Christle, holding reins of the horse-drawn wagon, operated a hauling business and was moving machinery when this picture was taken in about 1913. Christle's home at the corner of Third Street and Seventh Avenue SE is in the background. In the middle is Christle's son, Joseph. (*Submitted by Don Christle, grandson of Joseph Christle*)

IN STYLE

Mrs. C. Evans of 710 17th Ave., Cedar Rapids, was elegantly dressed for her photograph sometime before World War I. (*African American Historical Museum and Cultural Center of Iowa photo*)

WEDDING DAY

Carrie Christle and Wencil Bena and their attendants are shown on their wedding day in Cedar Rapids in November 1914. (*Submitted by Dorothy Nemecek*)

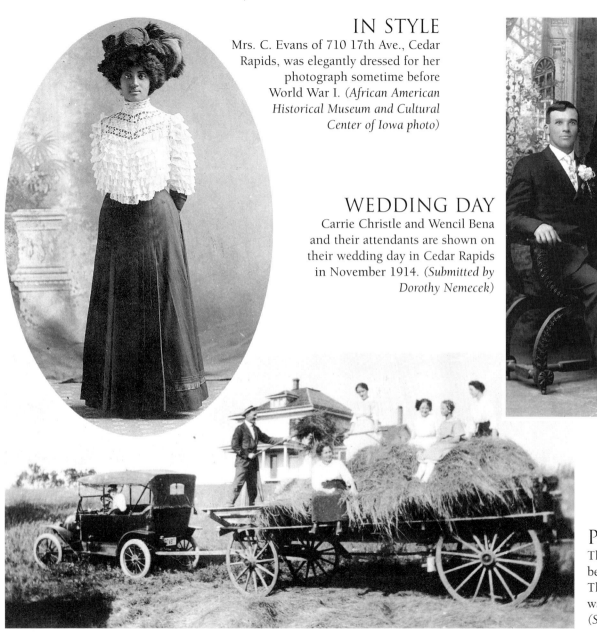

PARTY TIME

This group of hayrack riders seems to be very well-dressed for the activity. The photo is dated about 1913 and was taken in Linn County. (*Submitted by Sheila Streight*)

HOME DELIVERY

William Aossey Sr. sold a variety of items from his wagon – some food items, pots and pans, overalls and boots, sewing materials and some fabrics and he always had hard candy for the children, according to his son. He traveled as far north from Cedar Rapids as Albert Lea, Minn. He's shown at a farm in 1914. The team and wagon were later replaced by a truck. He immigrated to America from Syria when he was about 16. He found work as a farmhand in Iowa. His first name, Yahya, was Americanized to William by his German immigrant employers. He next worked in a grocery store. Eventually he was able to use his savings to buy a horse and a wagon. (*Submitted by Annabell Weaver*)

WEDDING DAY

Arthur E. Johnson and Blanche Frink are pictured on their wedding day in 1914. They later lived at 718 Ninth Ave. SW. They met at St. Luke's Hospital after Johnson's legs were crushed while working for the railroad and Blanche was his nurse. A family member told how she was pushing his wheelchair down the hall at the hospital when he asked her to lean over. When she did he kissed her on the cheek. She was so flustered that she pushed the wheelchair forward into an open closet, knocking bed pans off the shelves. Johnson became a watch repairman. They were married for almost 50 years. (*Submitted by Louise Johnson*)

RIDING IN STYLE

John Vlasek of Cedar Rapids drives a Harley-Davidson motorcycle in Bever Park in about 1915. Riding in the sidecar is his wife, Mamye, and children, Elma and Albert. (*Submitted by Anna Mae Vlasek*)

IN THE DRIVER'S SEAT

Eugene Kelly (third from left) was a conductor on Cedar Rapids streetcars. The men are shown in 1915 in what is believed to be a control room for the cars located in a building on Second Street NE. Streetcar service between Cedar Rapids and Marion started in 1880. The cars were originally powered by steam but then electrified in 1890. The 1883 Cedar Rapids city directory points out that in the early years on the Marion route, horses were used in the city limits and a motor the rest of the way. Kelly was grandfather of the late Jim Barnes, assistant police chief. (*Submitted by Suzanne Barnes*)

OPEN FOR BUSINESS

Edward Killian arrived in Cedar Rapids in 1911 and purchased the Taft store on the corner of Third Street and First Avenue SE. Two years later, the store moved to this location at the corner of Third Avenue and Second Street SE, which would be the store's main home for the next 70 years. Killian's closed in 1982. (*Submitted by Vivian Rinaberger*)

WORKING ON THE RAILROAD

This railroad round-house crew was photographed in about 1915. The man shown fifth from the right in the second row is Otto Slapnicka Sr. Although several railroads had freight and passenger depots in Cedar Rapids at that time, only the Rock Island had shops here according to a 1915 city directory. *(Submitted by Sharon Thompson)*

SHOW TIME

The Johnson Elementary School orchestra is shown in 1915 or 1916 sitting on the sidewalk along Washington Avenue SE in front of the school. Today, Johnson School is at 355 18th St. SE. The 1910 building pictured was demolished to make way for the new school. *(Submitted by Vivian Rinaberger)*

BIG LIZZ

This 1915 photo shows the men who rode "Big Lizz" to fires just after the Cedar Rapids department started the transition from horse-drawn equipment to motorized trucks. The central fire station was at 214 Third St. NE, with seven full-time salaried men. Previously, fires were fought by a volunteer department. The switch to motorized equipment started in 1914 and was completed by 1919. *(Fire Department photo)*

YOUNG MEN AND THEIR FLYING MACHINE

This group of Linn County men is reassembling a Jenny plane, which probably means the photo was taken in the 1920s The location isn't known. (*Submitted by Don Milligan*)

OVER THERE

H. G. "Scoop" Forbes served in France and Germany during World War I as a member of Battery E of Cedar Rapids Iowa National Guard artillery unit. The United States entered the war in 1917. Treaties ending the war were signed in 1919. (*Submitted by Tom Forbes, son of H.G. Forbes*)

SHOW TIME – In 1915, this movie theater at 314 Third Ave. SE was the Strand. It later became the State and still later the World. Today the building, now called Nexus, is still used for entertainment purposes. (*Submitted by Vivian Rinaberger*)

WORKING TOGETHER

The Mentzer brothers built a house on N Street SW in about 1915. Left is John Mentzer. Charles Mentzer is at the right. Man in center is not identified. (*Submitted by Sheila Streight, great-granddaughter of John Mentzer*)

MAKING HAY

This crew is in a Linn County field probably in the early 1900s. They are picking up windrows. *(Submitted by Don Milligan)*

WAITING FOR TRAINS

Drivers and delivery wagons wait at the Union Depot in downtown Cedar Rapids in about 1915. They were waiting to load goods that had come in by train. *(Submitted by Bill Kuba)*

THE FAIR

Although the sign on the building clearly says the Franchere Company Department Store, the store was known as The Fair and was one of the first department stores in Cedar Rapids. It pretty much filled the 200 block of First Avenue NE and was owned by Napoleon Franchere. The Roosevelt is there today. This photo was probably taken in about 1915. (*Submitted by F&M Bank*)

BIG BUSINESS

The Sinclair Packing House was big business in early Cedar Rapids. T.M. Sinclair, a native of Ireland, was 29 in 1871 when he opened the plant at Third Street and 16th Avenue SE. He was only 38 in 1881 when he died in a fall at the plant. The Linn County History of 1878 described his business, which had between 300 and 450 employees as the most important in Cedar Rapids, the largest of its kind west of Chicago and the fourth largest packing house in the world. The plant was sold to Wilson and Co. in 1930. (*Gazette photo collection*)

FIGHTING FIRE

The Kimball Building at the corner of Second Avenue and Third Street was partially destroyed by fire in 1916. W.A. Reynolds Co., an insurance agent, was in the corner on the ground floor. Merchants National Bank was erected on this corner in 1925 and U.S. Bank is there today. The Cedar Rapids National Bank was across the street at 302 Second Ave. SE. Today that is the location of the drive-in bank and parking ramp. *(Submitted by Vivian Rinaberger)*

SPORTY REO

This 1916 photo shows members of the Harrison family ready for a ride in a REO. Paul R. Harrison stands in front of the car. James Harrison is in the driver's seat. REO cars and trucks were built by a company formed by Ransom E. Olds in 1904, the year he left Olds Motor Works. The last REO car was built in 1936; the last truck in 1975. *(Submitted by Donald Harrison, son of Paul R. Harrison and grandson of James Harrison)*

BRIDAL PARTY

Olga Suchomel and Charles John were married in Cedar Rapids on Sept. 30, 1916. They were attended by her sister, Blanche Suchomel, and his brother, Edward John. Charles John was killed May 22, 1919, when the Douglas Starch plant exploded. A total of 43 people died and windows were broken all over downtown. The plant was located where Penford is today, 1001 First St. SW. (*Submitted by Dorothy Nemecek*)

READY FOR CUSTOMERS

A total of 24 Studebaker cars arrived at Hogan Brothers in Marengo on Aug. 4, 1916. Black was the basic color. (*Submitted by Lewis Newman*)

BIRTHDAY PARTY

It was George Drummey's birthday in 1916 and his friends all came. The photo was taken in the living room at 1221 Third St. NW where the party was held. (*Submitted by John Gallagher*)

EYES FRONT

White shirts and ties appear to be required for boys attending St. Berchman's School in Marion. The photo was taken in 1916 in the private school's new assembly hall. The school, which opened in the late 1890s, was in a large house at the corner of First Avenue and South 15th Street. (*Submitted by Patricia Bilsland*)

PHOTO TIME

Jacob Hadish and his grandson, John J. Hadish, and the dog Flossie are shown outside Jacob Hadish's Iowa City home in about 1917. (*Submitted by Louise Hadish, wife of John Hadish*)

HISTORIC CORNERSTONE

The cornerstone of the house at 2111 Fifth Ave. SE reflects some of the history of the man who built the house, E.J.C. Bealer. His Civil War service was so important to him that he put the date of his enlistment, June 7, 1862, on the cornerstone. Bealer, once owner of the Cedar Valley Quarry between Tipton and West Branch, built the house in 1912. In 1924, he gave it to his daughter, Orphea Bealer Brimm, and her husband with the proviso that he be allowed to live there until his death. He died in 1928. Orphea Brimm died in 1959 and the house and land were donated to Cornell College. The house was purchased by Larry and Mary Ann Nelson in 1988. Bealer's quarry was in operation until about 1910 when the advent of Portland cement spelled the end to the need for stone. The three women on the steps in this 1920 photo are believed to be servants. "Aunt Gertie worked" is written on the back. (*Submitted by Mary Ann Nelson*)

STRIKE UP THE BAND

This "band," made up of employees from Killian's Department Store at the corner of Third Avenue and Second Street SE, in the background, was ready to lead a parade in 1918. On the back of the photo, John Stava, manager of Killian's annex, had written, "It is a fine 'combination,' no?" *(Submitted by Teresa Sopousek)*

PAYING TRIBUTE

The body of Victor Hahn, a veteran of the Spanish-American War, received a military escort when he died in 1918. His funeral procession down Main Street in Mount Vernon was long, as the photo shows. Hahn, a descendant of Daniel Seward Hahn, one of the first settlers in Linn County, was born on a farm south of Mount Vernon. *(Submitted by Joanne Havran, niece of Victor Hahn)*

OUT FOR SPIN

Ray "Red" Rowell is the driver. His passenger's first name is Gladys. The car is a Hudson according to the name on the side. The year is about 1918 and they are in Cedar Rapids. (*Submitted by Robert Rowell*)

DRESS UNIFORMS

Anna Stroff and her family lived at 1310 B Ave. NE. A fire station was next door. Three of the firemen, wearing their dress uniforms, posed with her in front of the station in 1918. Capt. Spencer sits in the chair. Stroff's nephew remembers the brass pole the firemen used to slide down and how he and his brother almost got run over by the horses once when they left the station. (*Submitted by William Neff, nephew of Anna Stroff*)

READY FOR WORK

George N. Rowray stands alongside the truck he used in his delivery service in Cedar Rapids in 1918. He transferred baggage from trains. (*Submitted by Jack Rowray*)

PROUD FOREMEN

The sign in the background says it all. The year is 1919 and the men are foremen for the Cedar Rapids Mills of National Oats on 16th Street NE. We know the identities of three. William "Bill" Michalek is sixth from left in the back row; Frank Sullivan is third from the left in the front row; and Ben Dietz is third from the right in the front row. At the time, Michalek and Sullivan didn't know that they would later be related by marriage. Years later, Michalek's son, Charlie, 6 at the time, married Sullivan's daughter, Dorothy, then 5. (*Submitted by Carole Gauger, daughter of Charlie and Dorothy Michalek*)

WORK DAY

John Sherman Milligan works on his farm in Linn County in 1918. He built a new house and farm buildings in 1916. (*Submitted by Vern and Don Milligan*)

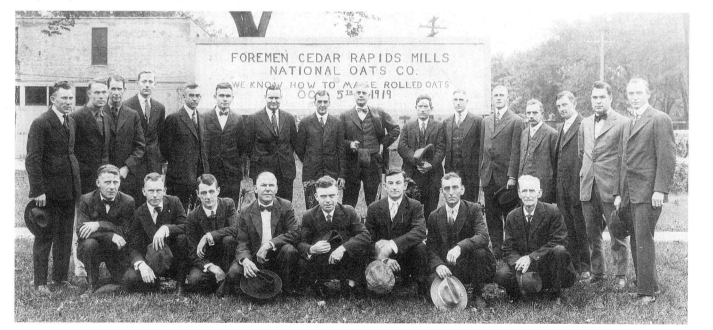

FRIENDS

Walter R. Stephenson of Cedar Rapids (right) and Jim Stephenson of Waterloo were in Des Moines for orientation in the U.S. Army in 1919. When the sergeant called the name "Stephenson" they both stepped forward. They became friends and served together in Washington, D.C. Treaties ending World War I were signed that year. (*Submitted by Betty Mineck*)

EGGS AND MORE

A Wilson and Co. processing plant for poultry, eggs and butter was on the grounds of the T.M. Sinclair packinghouse, Third Street and 16th Avenue SE, in about 1919 when this photo was taken. In 1930, Sinclair was sold to Wilson and Co. T.M. Sinclair opened in Cedar Rapids in 1871. The work crew in this photo taken in the early 1930s included Walter Potter (top row, far right) and Helen Potter (top row, third from left). (*Submitted by Ralph Potter, son of Walter and Helen Potter*)

BLAST RUINS

A blast blamed on dust leveled Douglas Starch Works and killed 43 employees on May 22, 1919. The blast also broke windows in many downtown stores. The plant, at Eighth Avenue SW and the Cedar River, was sold and eventually rebuilt by Penick and Ford. Penford is on that location today. (*Submitted by Berniece Shover*)

DELIVERY DAY

New Process Laundry at 116-124 Third St. NE was a busy place in the early 1900s, if the combination of horse-drawn wagons and delivery trucks are an indication. The building to the left later housed Danceland Ballroom on the second floor. Note the sign over the door: Suits, sponged and pressed for 50 cents; French Dry, cleaned and pressed for $1.50. (*Submitted by Vivian Rinaberger*)

SONG TIME

Frank Deming Cargin and his wife, Hazel, at piano, sang duets for Sunday evening entertainment. Picture may have been taken in the 1920s. Their address was listed as 1247 Fourth St. SW in an early city directory. (*Submitted by Sheila Streight*)

SCHOOL DAYS

Edina Donohue stands with her students at the small red-brick Dairydale School in 1920. At the time, Dairydale was in the county but the location was at the northeast corner of what today is Mount Vernon Road and 34th Street SE. Students in front row: Carl Van Antwerp, Beryl Wood, Marie Kaylar, Allan Nelson, Lumir Stolba, Pluma Terrill and Harold Bean; second row: Ernest Wood, Joe Nelson, Walter Woolridge, Ferman Clark, John Grow, Frank Pachta, Marvin Nemecek and Viola Kaylar; third row (only six of the students in this row were identified): Ronald Prior, Lucille Manson, Mae Woolridge, Mae Zrudsky, Mable Van Antwerp and Elmer Nemecek. (*Submitted by Dorothy Nemecek, wife of Marvin Nemecek*)

AT CONVENTION

Members of the Dramatic Order of the Knights of Khorassan are shown at a 1921 convention in Chattanooga, Tenn. The Cedar Rapids group was the Ardekan Temple No. 234 of the Knights of Pythias. Members called themselves DOKIES. An annual Christmas party at the children's home was one of their philanthropic activities. Ray Rowell is sitting at the right end of the front row. (*Submitted by Robert Rowell, son of Ray Rowell*)

READY TO RIDE

Motorcycle riders are shown in the early 1920s in front of the office for The Republican and Evening Times newspapers at 328 Third St. SE. The Evening Gazette purchased The Republican in 1927. (*Submitted by Jean Doran*)

COE IN 1922

Students and faculty gathered on the Coe College campus for this photo. Old Main is the building to the right. Built in two sections in 1868 and 1884, it was demolished in 1972 to make way for the Dows Fine Arts Center. Sinclair Chapel, built in 1910, is on the left. It burned in 1947. Today's Sinclair Memorial Chapel opened in 1951. First Avenue can be seen in the background between the two buildings. The well-dressed group reflects the dress code enforced at the time for both male and female students. (*Submitted by Chris McGee*)

WOMEN'S GAME

Members of the Coe College women's basketball team are pictured in 1902.

MAY FETE

The dancers are performing during the Coe College May Fete in 1923, presented by the women's physical education classes.

TIME FOR A SONG

The 1944 Coe College yearbook, The Acorn, was dedicated to the men in the Coe 22 group. This photo, showing them grouped around a piano, was on the dedication page. The Coe 22, all from the class of 1944, were called to active duty in April 1943. They went to basic training in California, then returned to Coe to wait for openings in Officer Candidate School at Fort Benning, Ga. That call came Jan. 1, 1944, and they were commissioned as second lieutenants in the Army infantry in May. All 22 were sent to the European Theater. Many were wounded; two were taken prisoner by German troops. Only one, Donald Niggemeyer, was killed. A platoon leader, Niggemeyer was on night patrol in Germany when he stepped on a land mine and was killed Oct. 26, 1944. (*Photos submitted by Coe College*)

STREET SCENE

This was the view of the 500 block of First Avenue NE in 1921. The multi-story building at the left is the YMCA. The two-story brick house would later make way for an addition to the YMCA. That expanded building was demolished in 2004 after a new YMCA opened at 207 Seventh Ave. SE. An office building is going up at this location. *(Submitted by Vivian Rinaberger)*

DELIVERY TIME

Ed Kacer was an employee of the Lagomarcino-Grupe Co., located at 327-329 First St. SE in 1922. The company was a wholesaler of fruits, nuts and oysters. *(Submitted by Kay Mosclip)*

PHOTO OP

Puggy Dewitt, Peanut Spurgeon and Bill Morgan are part of the group of men seated or standing around the car. H.G. "Scoop" Forbes stands on the car. Note the wooden spokes in the wheels. The year is about 1922, and they are in downtown Cedar Rapids. *(Submitted by Tom Forbes, son of H.G. Forbes)*

READY TO PADDLE
Otto Gundling of Cedar Rapids appears to be getting ready to go for a canoe ride on the Cedar River in 1923. (*Submitted by Arlene St. Clair*)

SUNDAY BEST
The congregation of the Bethel African Methodist Episcopal (AME) Church gathered for a photo in the early 1920s. The minister was the Rev. C.R. Waters. The church is at 512 Sixth St. SE. (*African American Historical Museum and Cultural Center of Iowa photo*)

WINTER SMILES
Alice Kolda, 9, and her sister, Louise Kolda, 12, stand next to their garage at 800 10th St. SE during the winter of 1923. They are now Alice Yanecek and Louise Hadish. (*Submitted by Louise Hadish*)

GRANT WOOD AND FRIENDS

Grant Wood and other faculty members posed for a photo on the steps of McKinley Junior High School on the day of the faculty breakfast in June 1923. Grant is in the front row, third from right wearing glasses. Math teacher Catherine Motejl is at far left of back row, in front of window; spelling and penmanship teacher Rose Waterstradt is fourth from left in back row in front of doorway. Wood painted "Arbor Day" in 1932 on commission from the school district in memory of Motejl and Waterstradt. Wood taught in Cedar Rapids for seven years, first at Jackson, then at McKinley. (*Cedar Rapids Community School District archive photo*)

IOWA ART COLONY

Grant Wood (right) established a summer art colony at Stone City in 1932. He's shown here in Stone City in 1933 with John Steuart Curry, regional artist from Kansas. The Depression killed the colony in 1934. That year Wood, who was a national figure by then, was hired to teach at the University of Iowa. He spent the last seven years of his life there, dying Feb. 12, 1942, just two hours short of his 51st birthday. (*Gazette photo collection*)

PRESIDENT'S TRAIN – The train carrying the body of President Warren G. Harding traveled across the country in 1923 from California, where he died Aug. 2, to Washington, D.C., for the funeral. It drew a large crowd when it went through Cedar Rapids. Greene Square is in the background. The first Washington High School is at the back. Notice the honor guard lined up on both sides of the railroad tracks. *(Submitted by Vivian Rinaberger)*

KEEPING PEOPLE WARM

This was the work force at Holland Furance Co., 1714 F Ave. NE, on Sept. 3, 1924. Edward Stepanek is 13th from right in the front row, holding his hat in front of him. *(Submitted by Ellen Colony)*

READY FOR BUSINESS

John S. Forbes used this Model T Ford in his business, Apex Repairs & Service at 824 Third Ave. SW. Photo was taken in 1924. *(Submitted by Tom Forbes, grandson of John Forbes)*

SPECIAL DELIVERY

Albert Vedder, driver for Lynch Transfer of Cedar Rapids, made deliveries all over the area, going as far as Chicago. This load in 1924 appears to be phonographs. In the background is the Cedar Rapids Public Library at the corner of Third Avenue and Fifth Street SE. (*Submitted by Jean Doran*)

DRIVE TIME

Betty Jean Stephenson (Mineck),
3, was out for a drive in the
neighborhood in 1924. Her family
lived at 1710 First Ave. NW.
(*Submitted by Betty Mineck*)

ALWAYS IN STYLE

These two photos of Libbie Nechville Kula of Cedar
Rapids were taken in the 1920s. She graduated from
Washington High School in 1919. Commencement was
held at Greene's Opera House. Her family still has the
book she kept from her high school days. One of the items
was a copy of a newspaper story describing how the girls
attending Washington and Grant Vocational School
would in the future wear blue uniforms trimmed in black
braid and buttons. (*Submitted by Kathy Carnahan*)

PLAYING DOLLS
Jane Rice (left), 5, and her friend Leora Marshall play with dolls in this 1924 picture taken in the 1500 block of C Avenue NE. (*Submitted by Jane Rice Helgeson*)

IN CONTROL
Bob and LuVerne Wheeler of Cedar Rapids hold the reins as they get ready for a ride in this 1925 photo. (*Submitted by Roger Techau*)

SUITED UP
Members of the 1925 Quaker Oats Co. baseball team pose for a picture probably taken at Daniels Park in northeast Cedar Rapids. The team was part of the eight-team M and J League that played games at the park. (*Submitted by Don Buchheister*)

COURTHOUSE STEPS

Members of the Iowa Sheet Metal Contractor's Association gathered on the steps of the new Linn County Courthouse in 1925. Ethel Gundling, eighth from left in the front row, is the mother of Arlene St. Clair, who submitted the photo. Her father, Otto, is fifth from left in the fourth row. Members of the Ilten family are also in the photo. Moving of the courthouse to Cedar Rapids ended a long fight with Marion over the location of the seat of county government. *(Submitted by Arlene St. Clair)*

READY FOR ACTION

The crew of Cedar Rapids Hose House No. 2 at 503 Fifth St. NW are pictured around 1925. Men believed to be stationed there at the time were Fred Simon, George Stephen, Emory Milikan, Charles Usher and Joe Stanek. *(Submitted by Bill Kuba)*

OUT OF MUD

The Wm. Horrabin Construction Co. of Mount Vernon helped get Iowa drivers on paved roads in about 1925. A crew, which includes Paul and James Harrison of Cedar Rapids, work on Lincoln Heights Drive SE, part of old Highway 30 and the Lincoln Highway. (*Submitted by Donald Harrison*)

FIRST JURY FOR NEW COURTHOUSE

Posing on the front steps of the new Linn County Courthouse in 1925 are members of the first jury drawn after the move into the new building. Bottom row (from left): T.A. Yocum, F.A. Parcel. F.A. Rowe, Mrs. C.J. Stewart, G.A. Perkins, V.V. Bartlett. Top row (from left): Judge F.O. Ellison, Mrs. B.R. Abbey, Mrs. Clyton Crull, Mrs. R.L. Jensen, Mrs. E.R. Kauppe, P.J. Laffan, W.H. Hoover and Richard Preston, bailiff. (*Submitted by Cedar Rapids Scottish Rite Masons*)

PLAY IT AGAIN

Player pianos were popular at the music store operated by Francis W. Slapnicka at 211 Second St. SE in 1925. The shelves to the left are crowded with rolls of music. Young man in front of the counter is Otto Slapnicka Sr. (*Submitted by Sharon Thompson and Barbara Stotler, granddaughters of Otto Slapnicka*)

SUCCESSFUL HUNT

Howard Klemer, William Michalek and Sam Mulligan show off their birds in the fall of 1926. They were at the Michalek home at 1060 32nd St. NE, Cedar Rapids. *(Submitted by Carole Gauger)*

PICNIC GATHERING

Members of Salem Church gathered in 1926 for a picnic. The only person identified is Albert Vedder, one of the young men standing in the back row. The church today, known as Salem United Methodist, is at 225 First Ave. SW. *(Submitted by Jean Doran)*

ON THE ROAD

Dewey Alexander (left) was a long-time employee of the Linn County Road Department. Other man in this photo from the 1920s is unidentified. Alexander lived in Cedar Rapids. (*Submitted by Kathy Carnahan*)

ROOSEVELT CREW

This crew of men helped build the Roosevelt Hotel at the corner of First Avenue and Second St. NE in 1926. Hotel opened Aug. 15, 1927. Most of the financing for the project was from Chicago investors, including Edith Rockefeller McCormick. Photo was taken by William Baldridge, an early Cedar Rapids commercial photographer. The hotel was named for Theodore Roosevelt, U.S. president from 1901 to 1909. (*Submitted by Bill Kuba*)

PLAY BALL

Ella Lansing owned Lansing Drug Co. at 416 N. 13th St. (Center Point Road). The store, across the street from Coe College, sponsored a baseball team. Shown in this 1926 photo are (from left) Louie Sanders, William Lansing, Wilmer Hendrickson, Jimmie Jirinec, Dave White and Donald Wernimont. *(Submitted by Harriet McDermott, sister of William Lansing)*

READY FOR WINTER FIRES

This 1926 photo of a Cedar Rapids firetruck and crew must have been taken in the winter, since there are chains on the truck's tires. Firemen are (from left) Milo Grubhoffer, "Boots" Stastny, Capt. Wencil Pohorsky and Jerry Cabalka. Photo was taken at 1111 Third St. SE at Hose Co. No. 4. *(Submitted by Bill Kuba)*

FILL ER UP

Paul R. Harrison stands in front of his Skelly Oil Co. station at the southwest corner of First Street and Eighth Avenue SW. The Tagolene gas pumps were gravity flow. The station lives on today as the Flying Wienie. (*Submitted by Dr. D.A. Paulson*)

Birds-Eye View of Rock Island Shops Cedar Rapids, Iowa

CEDAR RAPIDS RAIL YARDS

Cedar Rapids was a rail center when this panoramic photo was taken in 1927 by commercial photographer William Baldridge looking north from the top of a Quaker Oats elevator. The Rock Island Roundhouse is the largest. To the right of the Rock Island is a roundhouse for the Chicago North Western. In the foreground to the right are smaller shops for the Milwaukee and Illinois Central. The Cedar River is to the left. What later became Cedar Lake is in the background. The top of National Oats can be seen in the trees behind the water. The smokestacks of the Iowa Railway and Light Co. Power House are in the foreground. Houses to the right are part of what was called "Little Mexico." *(Submitted by Jeff Moser for Cargill and Leland Regel)*

READY TO HELP

Lionel Walker, a street-car motor man, stands by the steps of his car on the First Avenue bridge over the Cedar River around 1930. Notice that the street is brick. *(Submitted by Bill Kuba)*

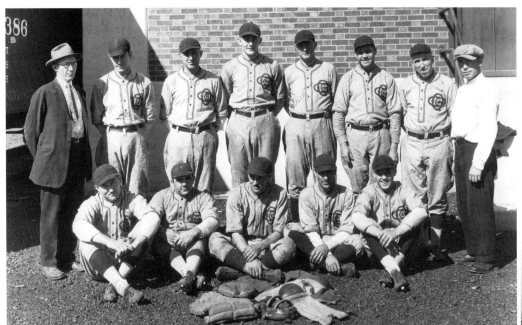

SADDLE UP

In 1928, Frank John's harness shop at 48 16th Ave. SW was one of two harness makers in Cedar Rapids. The Saddle and Leather Shop is at that address today. One of the original glass display cases is still in use. (*Submitted by Dorothy Nemecek*)

READY KILOWATT

The symbol on the shirts identifies these players as the Iowa Electric Co. team in 1928. The team was part of the M and J League that played at Daniels Park in northeast Cedar Rapids. There were eight teams in the league. The initials stand for Manufacturers and Jobbers and most factories at the time had a team. Most players were employees but sometimes summer jobs might be found for good high school players so they could suit up. (*Submitted by Don Buchheister*)

RIVER CRUISE

The Laura J and her passengers appear to be ready for what may have been a July 4 parade on the Cedar River in the 1920s. A railroad bridge is in the background. (*Submitted by Bill Kuba*)

A HAT-WAVING DAY

Sam Armstrong of Armstrong Clothing Co. in Cedar Rapids sent the first Airborne Express Letter from Cedar Rapids to Chicago on July 10, 1928. He stands in the middle of the group, holding his hat. The uniformed driver of the truck that delivered the letters and packages to the airport was DeVerne Hersom. The plane is shown in the background. As the second picture shows, after the plane took off, everybody attending waved their hats in the air. (*Submitted by Grace Ebert, daughter of DeVerne Hersom*)

DEFINITELY GRAND OPENING

The line of people waiting to help inaugurate the Capitol Theatre on Sept. 1, 1928, was at least four abreast and circled left around the building. The marquee advertised sound pictures, a stage show and a mighty organ. In 1929, The Capitol was purchased by Paramount Studios and renamed the Paramount. This photo was taken by William Baldridge, commercial photographer of the time. (*Submitted by Ray and Bonnie Bubke*)

TEACHER'S FIRST CAR

Katherine Kula Cook, sitting on the car's fender at right, bought this car in 1929. It was second hand and cost $165. A 1926 graduate of Washington High School, she taught in a number of area schools. One of her first jobs was as an elementary teacher at Frozen Hill, a country school near Prairieburg. She also taught at Story Flats, Castle Grove and Prairieburg Public. In the country schools, she would teach all eight grades. At Prairieburg, she taught the lower grades. She helped pay for high school by working for several families including the Sutherland Dows family as a nanny and general household helper. She received room and board. She completed what was called normal training in high school as preparation to teach. (*Submitted by Kathy Carnahan, daughter of Mrs. Cook*)

FORD PROMOTION

This photo and the one at the right, were two of a group of 28 photos mostly of owners and their trucks put together in 1929 by a salesman for Rude Ford and Lincoln Dealership at 511-525 Second Ave. SE as a marketing and advertising tool. J.E. Dulin was owner of The Highland Grocery and Market, 216 13th St. NW. Photos were taken by William Baldridge, commercial photographer. (*Photos submitted by Robert Hurych*)

HANDY SHOPPING

Early Cedar Rapids had many small grocery stores scattered about the city. Hanover Grocery and Market was at 315 13th St. NE. Frank Hanover was owner, and the family lived behind the grocery store.

SCHOOL FUN

A spring day in 1929 brought four Cedar Rapids high school students outside of Washington High School on Fourth Avenue SE across from Greene Square. They are Mary Dvorak, Anna Dvorak, Olga Zelenda and Stella Kubec. (*Submitted by Jan Aldrich*)

NO TRAINS TODAY

This was the scene at the Rock Island Roundhouse in March 1929 when the Cedar River flooded. The roundhouse was located in the rail yards behind Quaker Oats.

THE FLOOD OF 1929

F AVENUE LAKE

This was what F Avenue NW looked like during the 1929 flood. Hawkeye Lumber can be seen on the right, the location today of Cooper's Mill restaurant. Swiss Valley Farms is on the left side of the street today. *(Photos submitted by Bill Kuba)*

NO SCHOOL TODAY

A car chugs through the high water in front of Madison School at Third Street and Second Avenue SW in March 1929. The spring flood was blamed on snowmelt and heavy rains. (*Submitted by Elmer F. Grissel*)

COMING THROUGH

Two men in a rowboat are followed by a high-bodied car near the corner of First Street and Third Avenue SW during the 1929 flood. The Gatto Building at left was at 102-104 Third Ave. SW. People's Bank was on the corner at left and Fisher Drug Store on the corner next to the Gatto Building. Record flooding was blamed on a combination of snowmelt and rain. The water came up rapidly and some flooding started March 13. Floodwaters didn't go down until March 20. A record for the time, floodwaters hit 20.1 feet. (*Submitted by Bill Kuba*)

CHRISTMAS GATHERING

Anna and Albert Suchomel of 1420 L St. SW, their eight children, spouses and grandchildren are shown Christmas Day 1929. Some of the girls hold dolls. Old Van Buren School is in the background. (*Submitted by Dorothy Nemecek*)

POSING PRACTICE

Art students stand on the front steps of Warde Hall on the Mount Mercy College campus in 1929. Mount Mercy was still an all-women's college at this point. Male students were admitted for the first time in July 1969. (*Mount Mercy College photo*)

CAPITOL CAME FIRST

John Kelly of Cedar Rapids stands on Third Avenue SE downtown. In the background are the Capitol Theatre and the Killian Department Store. The Capitol opened Sept. 1, 1928, with great fanfare. The marquee claims that Anne Nichols' play is greater on the screen. The theater was soon purchased by Paramount Studios and renamed. At the time, Paramount Pictures was advertising movies with talking sequences. (*Submitted by Suzanne Barnes*)

BABY PARTY
Children born at Mercy Hospital (now Mercy Medical Center) and their mothers celebrate at the Second Annual Baby Party on May 11, 1929. The group is gathered at the hospital's former Sixth Avenue SE entrance. Pictured are Sister Mary de Lellis Welch (left center) and Sister Mary Visitation Touhey (upper right). Both sisters were nurses and veterans of World War I.
(*Mercy Medical Center photo*)

OPENING DAY
Colonial Baking Co. opened in Cedar Rapids on April 11, 1929, in a brick building at the corner of Fifth Avenue and Eighth Street SE. Jack Walsh, fifth from left in the back row, was the plant manager. This photo of employees was one of several taken that day.
(*Submitted by Harlan Witte*)

LET'S DANCE – Linger Longer was owned by Ernest and Buehla Henecke and was located

LET'S DANCE – Linger Longer was owned by Ernest and Buehla Henecke and was located next to their home at 2500 Zika Ave. NW. The dance floor was built in sections as the Heneckes could afford it starting in 1927; the roof was tar paper. The dance floor was open Thursdays and Saturdays. The cost on Thursdays was 25 cents for women and 35 cents for men. Saturday's charge was 35 cents for women and 50 cents for men. Music was provided by live bands such as Louis DeKlot, Stonekings Orchestra and Dad and his Boys. There was a beer garden on the right side between the house and the pavilion. The Henecke family sold both the pavilion and the house in 1944. The new owner changed the pavilion name to Mayview. (*Submitted by Harold Henecke*)

SITTING PRETTY

Sisters Mildred and Mary Gillen are shown in Shaver Park at Shaver Road and J Avenue NE in the 1930s. (*Submitted by Mary McEniry, daughter of Mildred Gillen Kruse*)

FUTURE HOME OF WARRIORS

This 1930 photo shows the farm of Edward Seitz. Today it is the location of Washington High School at 2205 Forest Dr. SE. The school was constructed in 1957. (*Submitted by Jeanne Jontz*)

SERIOUS BUSINESS

From the expressions on the faces of students in first and second grades at St. Patrick's School, posing for a picture is serious business in 1932. Robert Gatto is third from the left in the back row. *(Submitted by Patricia Bilsland)*

HONORS EARNED

The hats indicate that all of these men have earned the designation as 33rd Degree Masons of the Ancient and Accepted Scottish Rite. The man in the front row with the lapel ribbon who was on hand for the Nov. 13, 1931, event is the Sovereign Grand Inspector General Active 33rd Degree. They are standing on the steps of the Scottish Rite Temple at the corner of A Avenue and Sixth Street NE. The building was erected in 1927. *(Submitted by Cedar Rapids Scottish Rite)*

EASTER SUITS

Brothers Bob and Tom Rowell were ready for the Easter Parade on March 27, 1932. They are standing in front of their home at 349 Sixth Ave. SW. (*Submitted by Robert Rowell*)

OPEN FOR BUSINESS

Wency Gatto stands in front of Gatto's Grocery at 837 Third Ave. SW in 1933. This was one of four Gatto grocery stores. (*Submitted by Patricia Bilsland*)

COUNTRY TIME

The Wyoming Wranglers from Wyoming, Iowa, are getting in tune to play on KWCR in Cedar Rapids in 1932. Pictured are (from left) Durb Vargason, Mr. Davis, Archie Vargason, Walt Vargason and Kermit Usher. They performed in the area for several years. (*Submitted by Maycel Finkle, daughter of Archie Vargason*)

FIRST MOSQUE – This was the scene in 1934 when the mosque, the first place of worship specifically designed and built as a mosque in North America, opened in Cedar Rapids. Families gathered on the steps to be photographed by William Baldridge, well-known photographer of the time. Planning for the mosque had started in 1929 but the Depression delayed the project. The first immigrants, many of them from Syria, had arrived in Iowa in the early 1900s. Families in the photo are those of the following: Hussein Allick, Abdoo Aossey, Muhammed Aossey, Haj Yahya Aossey, Haj Zine Aossey, Najeeb Bedra, Cassim Bedra, Mir'ee DeHook, Haj Abbas Habhab, Ali Habhab, Mussa Habhab, Yusef Habhab, Ahmad Hamed, Haj Hussein Hamed, Kamel Hind, Emil Hobel, Hassan Igram, Haj Hassan Khalil Igram, Abdo Kallel, Hussein Killel, Hassan Murray, Haj Abdo Omar, Ali Sheronick, Haj Mahmoud Sheronick, Mahammed Sheronick, Khalil Sheronick, Mustapha Telb and Abdul Ghanny Thiher. Today, this structure at 1335 Ninth St. NW is known as the Mother Mosque in North America. A new mosque, The Islamic Center of Cedar Rapids at 2999 First Ave. SW, was built in 1971. The reference Haj in front of a name means the person has made the trip to Mecca. (*Submitted by Islamic Center*)

BEFORE REFRIGERATORS

Blocks of ice for ice-boxes were a necessity in the early years. James Lee Jarboe stands in front of the ice truck in 1934. His son, Walter, is on the porch of the house on C Avenue NW. Photo was taken by William Baylis, early commercial photographer in Cedar Rapids. (*Submitted by Dolores E. Jarboe*)

READY FOR CUSTOMERS

Ginsberg's was at 212 First St. SE (currently Alliant Tower) when this photo was taken in 1935. Isadore Ginsberg is in front, with a salesman, Dave Harris, behind him. The store was located here from 1930 to 1935. (*Submitted by Herman Ginsberg*)

NECESSARY PROJECT

Fred Langhurst (right) is part of a two-man crew building an out-house in rural Linn County in 1933. (*Submitted by Carly Langhurst, great-granddaughter of Fred Langhurst*)

ON STAGE

Edith Reed Atkinson and her brothers, Cecil and Wallace Reed, performed as the Gold Flashes dance trio from 1935 to 1944. Edith and Cecil are on stage here in about 1935. Edith, who was trained as a classical singer, later had a radio show on WMT and for 30 years was choir director at the Bethel African Methodist Episcopal Church. Cecil Reed started a Cedar Rapids floor service company in the 1940s and then in 1966 was the first Republican of African-American descent elected to the Iowa Legislature. The next year he was appointed Iowa employment security commissioner and then went on to a series of federal labor department posts. (*African American Historical Museum and Cultural Center of Iowa photo*)

CORNER GROCERY

In the 1930s Duster's Grocery Store was at the corner of 32nd Avenue and Oakland Road NE. It was owned by Leo and Marcella Duster. Leo and his brother Charles also owned several other grocery stores in Cedar Rapids. Note the Tagolene gravity flow gasoline pump in front of the store. The sign on the arch promotes milk-fattened poultry. In the 1940s, this building was leveled and replaced by Comb's Grocery. About 1950, the site was sold to Weaver Witwer, who operated Me-Too and Farm Market stores. Today, a Hy-Vee Food Store is at that corner. (*Submitted by John Duster, son of Leo and Marcella Duster*)

DEFINITELY ONE WAY

John S. Forbes stands alongside his car in this photo taken during the winter of 1936 west of Cedar Rapids. Heavy snowfalls occurred during January and February of that year. The plowed snow on the left is clearly higher than the car. (*Submitted by Tom Forbes, grandson of John Forbes*)

ROCK·ISLAND· BACK·SHOP CEDAR·RAPIDS·IOWA·AUG·11/36

BACK SHOP CREW FOR ROCK ISLAND

This group of men is identified as back shop workers at the Rock Island Roundhouse in Cedar Rapids in 1936. The roundhouse was the main repair facility in this area for the Rock Island. It was located in the yards area north of Quaker Oats. (*Submitted by Bill Kuba*)

WORKING ON THE RAILROAD

The size of the crew gives an indication of the importance of the Cedar Rapids roundhouse to the Rock Island Lines in the 1930s. Writing on the photo refers to this as the "first trick" roundhouse. The roundhouse, where engines were repaired, was located north of today's Alliant Energy power plant. One of the largest roundhouses in the state, it was in operation into the 1950s. (*Submitted by Don Buchheister*)

WORKING FOR LAPLANT CHOATE

Members of the hydraulics department at LaPlant Choate Manufacturing Co., 3015 First Ave. E, pose in the plant in September 1936. Allis-Chalmers was later at that location. There were company facilities on both sides of First Avenue. Dale Cornish is second from right. (*Submitted by Ruby and Doug Cornish*)

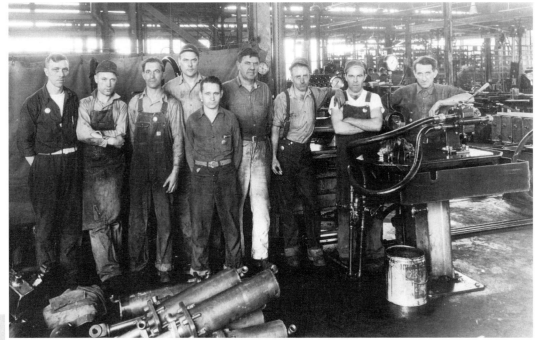

SHOPPING CENTER

This shopping area in the heart of the Oak Hill neighborhood was at Ninth Street and 12th Avenue SE in about 1936. From left are Krejci Bros. Grocery and Bakery, The Brown Derby tavern and Novak Barber Shop. (*Submitted by Sandra Rompot*)

PICTURE TIME

Students in the upper grades at Rosedale School No. 2 in rural Cedar Rapids gathered in October 1936 to have their picture taken. Teacher is Dorothy Schenken. Touch of Class Banquet Center is now in the building at 5977 Mount Vernon Rd. SE. (*Submitted by Dorothy Nemecek*)

SPLASHING GOOD TIME

Children from the Little Mexico neighborhood in northeast Cedar Rapids swim in Cedar Lake in about 1936. (*Submitted by Anthony Vasquez*)

FLYING HIGH

The name on the side of this Stinson SR-5 was The Cedar Rapids Gazette in 1937. Several people appear to be boarding. The plane is at Hunter Field, three miles south of Cedar Rapids. The field was opened in 1924 by Dan Hunter. Today, Bowling Street SW runs alongside where the field was and Gazette Communications' printing plant is on part of the site. *(Submitted by Carl Carson)*

GRADUATION DAY

Ready to face the world after graduation from McKinley High School in Cedar Rapids in 1936 are Helen Pleshek, Jane Rice and Mary Ellen McLeod. *(Submitted by Jane Helgeson)*

FRIENDS

Bob Clark (from left), Ardyce Lindsey, Betty Stephensen and Lynn Mineck are pictured in front of Stephensen's house at 1710 First Ave. NW in 1938. Betty and Lynn later married. *(Submitted by Betty Mineck)*

TAKING A DRINK

There really is a spring under the Spring House Restaurant, 3980 Center Point Rd. NE, and you can still sample the water by turning a faucet over a small pond inside the restaurant. This photo shows how McCloud Spring appeared in 1938 when it was still accessible to pedestrians. Sampling the water are Virginia Swallom (from left), Elva Swallom, Jeanne Booth, Emma Jakemit and Louise Swallom. In the 1840s, the plentiful water from the spring prompted John McLeod to locate a sawmill and gristmill there. Large amounts of watercress grew in the area, and people frequently took home bottles of water from the spring. The spring is capped today. *(Submitted by Louise Swallom McClurg)*

WORLD CHAMPS – Members of the YMCA's World Champion Boys Drum & Bugle Corps are shown on the steps of Roosevelt High School in 1938. Director was Ariel Cross from Marshalltown. Drum major was Billie Boston. Bugler Billie Dale, 9, at the right end of the top row, was the youngest member of the group. *(Submitted by William Dale)*

IT'S PICTURE TIME

Members of the Cedar Rapids Fire Department posed for a photo May 16, 1938, in front of the Central Fire Station at 427 First St. SE. The Science Station is there today. (*Submitted by Bill Kuba*)

SERVICE WITH A SMILE

The crew of A&W Root Beer at 1025 First Ave. SE lined up for a photo in 1938. (*Submitted by Dorothy Nemecek*)

MOBILE MESSAGES

Marjorie Sullivan Kessell (in car) drove this car her senior year (1939) at Franklin High School, 300 20th St. NE. She had her friends autograph the car. (*Submitted by Carole Gauger*)

SHOW TIME

The Roosevelt High School band poses on the steps of the school at 300 13th St. NW in 1939. (*Submitted by Lewis Newman, fourth from right in the third row*)

READY FOR ACTION

The Roosevelt High School football team of 1939 poses on the school field in northwest Cedar Rapids. Coach Wolf is on the right. A few of the members are identified by the numbers on their jerseys as follows: Lee Ilten (28), John Ensign (66), Dick Lewis (27), Fred Bissell (36), Mickey Mallory (24) and Martin Thorson (39). (*Submitted by Lewis Newman*)

READY FOR CUSTOMERS

The waitresses at the Maid-Rite Sandwich Shop at 1323 First Ave. SE lined up for a photo in 1940. They are identified only by first name: Dot, Maxine, Bert, Rose and Hazel. (*Submitted by Arlene St. Clair*)

STREET SCENE

This photo shows Second Avenue SE in the late 1940s. Globe Appliance is at 111 Second Ave. SE. *(Submitted by Kay Moscrip)*

SUNDAY BEST

The occasion isn't known but the women and children of Trinity Methodist Episcopal Church at 408 Third Ave. SW appear to be dressed in their Sunday best for this photo, which might have been taken around 1940. Pastor is J.P. Van Horn. *(Submitted by Bill Kuba)*

BIKES WERE HIS BUSINESS

Willard "Bill" Morgan (right, behind counter) and his brother-in-law Gus Dyson (left) are shown in Morgan Brothers Bicycles at 510 Third Ave. SE in 1939. The business was at that location from 1930 until 1962, when the building was leveled to make way for an addition to The Gazette next door. Morgan got a job in a bicycle shop in 1910 while still in elementary school. He kept that job for 10 years. Later, he and George Chambers were in partnership in a shop for four years. Then in 1925, Morgan and his brother bought a shop at 510 Fifth St. SE. They later moved to the Third Avenue location. Today, the shop is known as Northtowne Cycling and Fitness and is at 1150 Blairs Ferry Rd. NE. (*Submitted by Jane Stepanek*)

READY TO HELP

In 1941, the staff of the Paramount Theatre, 123 Third Ave. SE, included seven usherettes. Third from left is Betty Hermsen; eighth from left is Mary Edaburn. The three men at the right are the manager, a firefighter, and assistant manager. The movie playing was "Reap the Wild Wind," starring Ray Milland, John Wayne and Paulette Goddard. (*Submitted by Paul Fowler*)

LAB CLASS

These students are in the Mount Mercy College biology laboratory in 1941. The college had only female students at the time. Men weren't admitted as students until 1969. (*Mount Mercy College photo*)

WAITING FOR SANTA

Excited children wait for the Holiday Parade and Santa Claus at the corner of Second Street and Third Avenue SE sometime in the early 1940s. (*Submitted by Dick Bobenhouse*)

DELIVERY TIME

A load of new cars had just been delivered to Baxter Chrysler Plymouth at 829 Second Ave. SE in 1941. All employees were assembled to pose with the cars: two Plymouths are to the left; a Chrysler New Yorker Club Coupe is on the right. Gene Baxter, president and treasurer, is second from right. *(Submitted by Gene Baxter)*

PATRIOTIC PARADE

A parade to promote the sale of U.S. Savings Bonds brought out a crowd on this sunny day in 1942. The corner pictured is Third Avenue and Third Street SE. Liggett's Drugs is the location of today's Armstrong's Centre. Gov. Bourke B. Hickenlooper rode in an open white convertible. Cedar Rapids and Linn County set a national example in the number of war bonds purchased. Cedar Rapids was cited in October 1942 by the U.S. Treasury Department for outstanding achievement. A payroll deduction plan instituted in Cedar Rapids was used as a model elsewhere in the country. *(Submitted by Dr. D.A. Paulsen)*

FAMOUS HOOF

Charles Browning, Cedar Rapids blacksmith, shoes Roy Rogers' horse, Trigger, in 1942. Rogers stopped to see Roy Gaddis in Cedar Rapids during a cross-country trip and asked him to recommend a blacksmith. Browning was called and did the shoeing at the Gaddis home on First Avenue Road NW. He also put the first shoes on Trigger Jr. *(Submitted by Lewis Newman, stepson of Charles Browning)*

PATRIOTIC ACTION

Bert W. Rickard, a longtime employee of the Paramount Theatre, buys a U.S. War Bond in the lobby of the Paramount in 1942. Cedar Rapids was cited in October 1942 by the U.S. Treasury department for achievement in the sale of war bonds. Rickard, a stage electrician, previously had worked at the Majestic Theater and Greene's Opera House. *(Submitted by Ray and Bonnie Bubke)*

WELCOME TO CEDAR RAPIDS

Dorothy Cline, an employee of Iowa Manufacturing, was greeting a visitor to Cedar Rapids and Iowa Manufacturing in 1942. He had just gotten off the train at the Union Station downtown. *(Submitted by Jeanne Jontz, daughter of Dorothy Cline)*

ALL TOGETHER NOW

A chorus of Century Engineering employees are shown on May 6, 1943, singing during the ceremony in which Century received an Army-Navy E Award for production. Mary Jane Kenney of Cedar Rapids is at far right. During World War II Century manufactured aerial bomb fuses. This represented a big change for the company, which in 1939 was the largest manufacturer of oil heating units in the nation and had 150 employees. Wartime employment soared to about 900, many working 70-hour weeks. Sixty-five percent of those workers were women and 99 percent had never worked in a factory before. (*Gazette photo collection*)

WORKING FOR WAR EFFORT

In 1942, the Western Bohemian Fraternal Association of Cedar Rapids conducted a fund drive among members to buy ambulances for the U.S. Army. It eventually presented 12. This photo was taken in September 1942. Today the group is known as the Western Fraternal Association. (*History Center photo*)

VICTORY GARDENS

Three men stand in what appears to be several Victory Gardens in this undated photo from Cedar Rapids. They had a bumper crop of potatoes. (*History Center photo*)

PASSING IN REVIEW

Gov. Bourke B. Hickenlooper (third from left) was on the reviewing stand for an Easter Sunday war bond parade in Cedar Rapids on April 25, 1943. Joining him were (from left), Herbert E. Gaston, assistant secretary of the treasury; U.S. Secretary of the Treasury Henry Morgenthau Jr., Mrs. Hicklooper; Mrs. Harold Newcomb, Iowa women's chairman for war savings, and J.S. Young, president of the Federal Reserve Bank in Chicago. Morgenthau was in Cedar Rapids to praise the city's efforts in raising money through the sale of bonds. Hickenlooper, a Cedar Rapids attorney before his election as governor, later represented Iowa in the U.S. Senate for 24 years. While a senator he was a representative to the United Nations. He was a Republican. (*Gazette photo collection*)

EASTER DINNER

This photo taken at a family Easter dinner in 1943 is from the album of Nova Dannels. For years, Nova and Richard Dannels lived in a small Cape Cod home at the corner of Wilson Avenue and 29th Street SW. (*Gazette photo collection*)

PROUD EMPLOYEES

Employees of Iowa Manufacturing gather in front of the Cedar Rapids plant during the 1940s. The plant was honored with an Army-Navy E Award for production of the many rock crushers sent overseas during World War II to help rebuild roads. The woman standing just to the right of the man in the center of the first row is Dorothy Cline, a secretary at the company. (*Submitted by Jeanne Jontz, daughter of Dorothy Cline*)

FAREWELL

Howard "Pat" Gallagher was leaving for naval service in World War II when this photo was taken in front of Union Depot in Cedar Rapids in 1942. He poses with his brothers, John (in front), Don and Tom. They were the sons of Pat and Marie Gallagher of 1021 Fifth St. NW. The family lived behind the grocery store they operated at that location from 1922 into the 1960s. (*Submitted by John Gallagher*)

MANNING THE PUMPS

"Mac" Charles Eugene McCannon stands at the pump at McCannon's B-Square Service at 4825 Center Point Rd. NE in about 1943. The station was at the point where Highway 100 now crosses Center Point Road. *(Submitted by Richard E. Larson, grandson of "Mac" McCannon)*

ONCE MANSION HILL

This once grand residence at 625 A Ave. NE was originally the home of Mr. and Mrs. George Williams. Pictured in 1943, the house, one of many mansions in this area in the early years, was later torn down to make room for Baxter Motors Inc. There was a ballroom on the third floor. Wine glasses and other related items were found when the house was demolished. *(Submitted by Vern Ann Baxter)*

REUNION GATHERING

The Centesimal Reunion Class is shown on the steps of the Scottish Rite Temple at the corner of A Avenue and Sixth Street NE in October 1944. This was the 100th reunion of the Iowa Consistory. The number of members wearing military uniforms is a reminder that World War II was still going on. (*Submitted by Cedar Rapids Scottish Rite Masons*)

WILSON TEAM

All suited up and ready to go are members of the Wilson High School football team in 1944. Pictured are (from left) Bob Horsky, George Henderson, Bill Birkicht, Joe Blazek, Don Conway and Don Andrew. Today, Wilson at 3201 J St. SW, is a middle school. (*Submitted by Mary Newman*)

SPECIAL DELIVERY

The year was 1946 and employees of Cook's Paints were advertising a new store and delivering supplies in the 400 block of First Avenue SW with a horse-drawn wagon. (*Submitted by Mike Merrifield*)

READY FOR
HOLIDAY SHOPPERS

The staff of the Neisner variety store at 215 First
Ave. SE is shown during the holiday shopping season
in 1945. Mary Davis is at the back of the three
women standing behind the lunch counter on the
right side. The shopper's lunch special is advertised
at 20 cents. The store advertised prices starting at a
nickel. Coventry Gardens Mall is located there today.
(*Submitted by Teresa Davis, daughter of Mary Davis*)

THE WINNER

Judith Ann Nemecek was 2
years, 8 months old when she
won first prize in the Beauty and
Health Contest held in
conjunction with a savings bond
rally at Memorial Coliseum in
Cedar Rapids on Nov. 7, 1945.
(*Submitted by Dorothy Nemecek*)

HEADED FOR COLLEGE

University of Iowa co-eds are shown in the CRANDIC's Cedar Rapids depot at Second Street and Fourth Avenue SE in 1947. They are waiting for a train to Iowa City. Thousands of students used the passenger service until it ended in 1953. Usage hit a record 573,707 passengers in 1945. Declining usage after that was blamed on more affordable cars and better roads. The interurbans were heavily used in the years when Iowa was bogged down with mud roads. In fact, the CRANDIC between Cedar Rapids and Iowa City was a lifesaver for many after the Iowa-Minnesota game in 1922. A heavy rain had left all roads a sea of mud, and cars were stuck for miles. Some spent the night in their cars but others walked to the right of way of the interurban and waited for a train. After stranded fans were rescued, the railway ran flat cars out to help bring back the stuck cars. Passenger service ended in 1953. (*Crandic Photo*)

FIRST FLIGHT

Eight Cedar Rapids businessmen went by train to Chicago to get aboard the first United Airlines passenger plane scheduled to land at the Municipal Airport, initiating service here in 1947. The men were Gail Miller, Kenneth Hastie, John Baldridge, Earl Bapty, Paul Palmer, Oliver J. Swab, Gene Baxter and W.H. Wenkstern. The men boarded the plane in Chicago. (*Submitted by Gene Baxter*)

FAMILY REUNION

Pictures are part of all family reunions. Shown at Ellis Park in 1948 at left is Dorothy Banks. Mary Ann Banks is at right. Girl in middle isn't identified. *(Submitted by Mary McEniry)*

RIDE 'EM COWBOY

Mike Merrifield was ready to ride to the rescue in this 1948 photo taken in front of 413 First Ave. SW. He was pretending to be Hopalong Cassidy, cowboy movie star of the time, complete with "horse," hat and cigarette. *(Submitted by Mike Merrifield)*

LONGTIME LIBRARIAN

Ruby Taylor, a graduate of Coe College, was a librarian at the Cedar Rapids Public Library for 45 years. A descendant of a family that came to America on the Mayflower, she helped produce a book about Mayflower families. She is shown in the 1940s with her dog Ginger, a cocker spaniel. Ruby Taylor's father, Eugene, was a well-known architect in early Cedar Rapids. He died in 1924. *(Submitted by Teresa A. Davis)*

LARIMER FAMILY

The house at 2036 Fifth Ave. SE is known as the Ferguson-Larimer House in honor of the first two families who lived in it. Henry and Ella Ferguson built it in 1915 and lived here until 1920. The Edwin Larimer family, pictured in 1948, lived here the next 40 years until 1961. The Larimers operated a hardware store at 120 First St. SE. The house is part of the first Vernon Heights addition. Houses in this area were built to accommodate cars. This house was built with a drive-in garage with a car washing setup in the basement. The garage was reached from the alley. Both early families had servants and there are still remnants of the bell system used to summon them. The house, shown here today, has been refurbished by current owners John Cairns and Jim Foxwell. (*Submitted by John Cairns*)

FERGUSON
-LARIMER
HOUSE

CEDAR RAPIDS ROCKETS

The year was 1949, the first and only year for a baseball team called the Cedar Rapids Rockets. This group pictured in the Veterans Memorial clubhouse includes both team employees and boosters. Pictured are (from left) businessman Howard Hall, George Noble, Thurmy Harris, Bud Curran, Glen Matter, Alex Fidler and Dr. Eddie Anderson. The tall man in the back on the right is Bill Zuber of Amana, who pitched for the Yankees and the Red Sox. Kneeling is movie star and singer Dennis Morgan, who sang "The Star-Spangled Banner" before the game. Anderson was in his last year as University of Iowa football coach. Fidler was circulation manager for The Gazette. One man partially hidden in the back row could not be identified. *(Submitted by Don Buchheister)*

WINDOW SHOPPING

In 1949, Yager's department store was located at the corner of Second Avenue and Third Street SE. The U.S. Bank parking ramp and drive-in bank are at that corner today. *(Submitted by Marvin C. Kacer)*

HAPPY EVENT

On May 20, 1949, WMT and the Killian Co. marked 15 years of store sponsorship of radio newscasts. At the time, the continuous sponsorship was the second longest in radio history. Shown are (from left) Beulah Marsh, Killian's personal shopper on the program throughout its history; W.B. Quarton, general manager of WMT, who originally handled the account as a salesman; A.L. Killian, company president; and Douglas Grant, program director at WMT who presented the first of the newscasts. *(Submitted by Vivian Rinaberger)*

FLYING TRIP

Members of the Moose Club Girls Drum and Bugle Corps gathered for a picture in 1949 before boarding the plane in Cedar Rapids for San Francisco, where they performed and marched during a Moose Club convention. Jean Vedder Doran is fourth from left in the back row.
(Submitted by Jean Doran)

DERBY DAY

This was the scene for the 1949 Soap Box Derby on the hill near Kingston Stadium in west Cedar Rapids. Gene Baxter and Ed Wathan are second and third from the left. *(Submitted by Gene Baxter)*

CLIMBING HIGH

Kindergarten children are shown on the playground at old Taylor School at 500 Sixth St. SW in 1949. Teacher is Miss Wheeler. Today, Taylor School is at 720 Seventh Ave. SW, a few hundred feet to the west of where the old school was. *(Submitted by Mary McEniry)*

STREET MUSIC

John Lopez, Richard Mendoza and a friend play outside a store that may have been close to First Street and First Avenue NE where Cedar River Tower is today. The picture was taken in the late 1940s or early 1950s. (*Submitted by Anthony Vasquez*)

BATTER UP

Members of the Sanitary Dairy baseball team are shown in the 1950s. They played in the M & J League at Daniels Park in northeast Cedar Rapids. Front row (from left): Jersey Jermeier, Jim Bell, John Jenny, Ed Hipp and Don Buchheister. Back row (from left): Lee Mudd, Jim Josch, Gary Hilton, Lyle Pickart, unidentified. Bat boy is Dink Bruer. (*Submitted by Don Buchheister*)

LITTLE MEXICO

Lydia Rodriquez, one of Cedar Rapids' first Mexican residents, is shown in her garden at 317 Seventh St. NE in the neighborhood known as Little Mexico in the early 1950s. (*Submitted by Anthony Vasquez*)

BREAK TIME

Lydia Rodriquez's grandchildren take a break from playing in the back yard of her "Red House" at 317 Seventh St. NE in the early 1950s. The house, the only red one in the neighborhood, was a gathering place. Row 1 (from left): Jody Beltram, Alfonso Vasquez, Lydia Gonzalez; Row 2: Ben Vasquez, Nancy Beltram, Margaret Pena, Carmen Rodriquez; Row 3: Peggy Vasquez, Corrine Gonzalez. (*Submitted by Anthony Vasquez*)

BIG DAY

June 4, 1950, was the wedding day for Bessie Santas and Stavros Hadjiathanassiou. The bride and bridesmaids got together at her father's house at 1250 Fifth Ave. SE. The name was later shortened to Hadjis. (*Submitted by Demetrios Hadjis*)

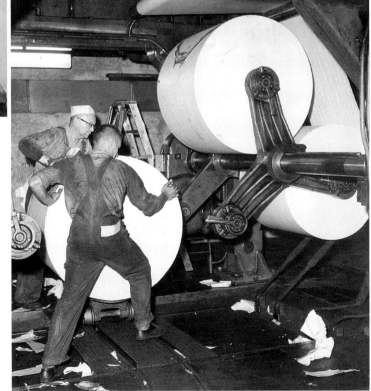

HEAVE HO

Loading rolls of newsprint onto The Gazette's letterpress in 1960 are Jerry Fleming (front) and Marty Kucera. The Gazette was founded in 1883. This press was in the building at 500 Third Ave. SE. (*Gazette photo*)

CRITERION CLUB

Members of this Cedar Rapids women's club were photographed in the 1950s. First row (from left): Esther Nance, Ann Turner, Vivian Smith, Mary Milton, Emma Turner. Second row (from left): Hattie Martin, Frances A. Baker, Lorena Hammond, Nina Woodson, Ethel Clark, Evelyn Reed, Hazel Smith. Third row (from left): Evelyn Jackson, Catherine Collins, Celestia Perkins, JoEtta Collins, Ellouise Brown. (*African American Historical Museum and Cultural Center of Iowa photo*)

LODGE GATHERING

The Prince Hall Grand Lodge of Iowa sat for a photo in about 1950. The man in the middle of the picture wearing a suit is William G. Reed. He moved his family, which included seven children, to Cedar Rapids from Illinois. He worked as a janitor at the old railroad depot. One of his children, Cecil Reed, went on to become the first African-American Republican elected to the Iowa Legislature in 1966. (*African American Historical Museum and Cultural Center of Iowa photo*)

BASKET TIME

This was the LaPlant Choate basketball team in 1951. Standing are (from left) Bill Faches, longtime Linn County Attorney; Jim Rice, Frank Kvach and Coach Bob Havlik. Havlik was a longtime policeman. In the front row (from left) are Don Buchheister, Bob Cooper and Ken Milsap. LaPlant Choate was located at 3015 First Ave. E. (*Submitted by Don Buchheister*)

HAPPY DAYS

This class from the Shueyville Elementary School was obviously happy with their field trip to the YMCA at the corner of Fifth Street and First Avenue NE in the spring of 1951. *(Submitted by Karen Millard)*

MODERN CABINS

The E and R Motel at the southwest corner of 16th Avenue and Edgewood Road SW boasted of having modern cabins for travelers in this 1952 photo. The cabins are shown at the left. *(Submitted by Terry Johnson)*

IN THE SWIM

Members of the Cedar Rapids synchronized swimming team, The Aquarelles, are shown in the 1950s at the Swimming Hall of Fame at Fort Lauderdale, Fla. The group was organized in 1957 by Beulah Gundling, a well-known swimming teacher. They were the only team in the United States performing aquatic routines composed entirely of floating patterns, patterns choreographed to demonstrate a theme and coordinated with music and costumes. They were inducted into the Swimming Hall of Fame after earning many top ratings at the International Festival of Aquatic Art. (*Submitted by Don Buchheister*)

WHISTLE-STOP

Richard Nixon, then a U.S. senator from California, was in Cedar Rapids on Oct. 10, 1952, campaigning as vice-presidential candidate on the Republican ticket headed by Dwight D. Eisenhower. His 20-minute visit to Cedar Rapids was part of a 24-hour whistle-stop tour through Iowa. An estimated 5,000 people jammed the Fourth Street NE area around the noon hour. Quaker Oats towers can be seen in the background of the photo showing him reaching down from the railcar's rear platform to shake hands. Photos were taken for The Gazette by John McIvor and Tom Merryman. McIvor recalls standing on the roof of the Chicago and Northwestern freight house to take the crowd photo. (*Submitted by John McIvor*)

BUD LINGEL
1952
RAY NOVOTNY
CLARENCE STUDT
BOB ZEMAN
BOB ERENBERGER
ORVAL UNASH
ALBERT BLOUNT

FLYING HIGH

Hunter Field was located at the corner of Highway 30 and Bowling Street SW for more than 30 years. Dan Hunter, who learned to fly when he was 18, paid $10 in 1924 to lease this field, which then was three miles south of Cedar Rapids. He built his own hangar and maintained his own plane. Three years later, he organized the Cedar Rapids Airways Corp. and offered flight instruction, charter trips and sold new and used aircraft. The field was in use until 1958, when Hunter retired and sold the land. Today, Gazette Communications' printing plant is on part of this land. *(Submitted by Carl Carson)*

LET'S DANCE

Bob Zeman's Iowa Rangers band of Ely were ready to play in 1952. From left: Bud Lingel, Ray Novotny, Clarence Studt, Bob Zeman, Bob Erenberger, Orval Unash and Albert Blount. *(Submitted by Robert Zeman)*

FIRST COMMUNION

Altar boys lead the first communion class into St. Patrick's Catholic Church, 510 First Ave. NW, on May 17, 1953. The boy behind the altar boy on the right is Mike Merrifield. Among those attending were two teachers at St. Patrick's School. Sister Mary Thomas is on the left. (*Submitted by Mike Merrifield*)

PARADE TIME

The 1953 Christmas parade moves in front of Haldy Beauty and Barber Supply Co. located on the ground floor of the ORC Building (Order of Railway Conductors) at 104 First Ave. NE. (*Submitted by Robert M.L. Johnson*)

POLICE PROOF

Tom Ecker left the University of Iowa campus after class on a Friday in 1954 and hitchhiked to Greenville, S.C., and back. Now of Cedar Rapids, Ecker said he was back in Iowa City by dark on Sunday. He offers this picture of himself talking to a Greenville policeman as proof. *(Submitted by Tom Ecker)*

RIDING HIGH

Becky Prignitz is having fun riding, probably at CeMar Acres, in about 1954. CeMar was an amusement park along First Avenue SE at the edge of Marion. *(Submitted by Arc)*

FIRST AIRPORT TERMINAL

The farmhouse shown here was the first passenger terminal for the Cedar Rapids Municipal Airport when service was initiated by United Airlines in 1947. A United DC-6B is shown on the tarmac. The farmhouse served as the terminal until it was replaced in the early 1950s. *(Gazette photo collection)*

CANADIAN BOMBER CRASHED IN CEDAR RAPIDS

On July 12, 1954, a Canadian Air Force Lancaster Bomber was making test runs over the Cedar Rapids Municipal Airport when it crashed as it approached for a landing. The plane burst into flames on impact and firefighters used foam to control the fire. Four crew members, including the pilot, scrambled to safety and suffered only minor injuries. The four-engine plane, the first Lancaster to land in Cedar Rapids, was here for the installation of two Collins Radio UHF transceivers and an antenna. The crew was to leave for home on the day the plane crashed. *(Submitted by Bill Kuba)*

PEDAL TIME

These four friends worked the split shift at Harmony Cafeteria, 118 Third St. SE, in 1954. During the two-hour break between shifts, they would rent bicycles built for two and head out. Sometimes they would go to Ellis Park and go swimming. From left: Darlene Dawson, Marilyn Conklin, Linda Milota and Shirley Klimes. They graduated from high school in 1954 and are still friends today. They are riding on Second Street SE. *(Submitted by Darlene Dawson)*

GOLF LESSON

Comedian Bob Hope and Gazette Sports Editor Gus Schrader were giving actress Marilyn Maxwell some golf pointers when this photo was taken in 1955 at the Cedar Rapids Country Club. Hope had appeared at a benefit for the Iowa County Hospital Fund in Marengo the day before and spent the night at the Roosevelt Hotel. He was invited to play golf by some country club members. (*Gazette photo*)

READY FOR NFL

Edward Sterling Langhurst III was 3 when this photo was taken in 1955. When his brother and his friends came home from football practice at Washington High School, they would dress Eddie in their gear. Eddie loved to be like the "big" boys. (*Submitted by Carly Langhurst, daughter of Edward Langhurst*)

BALANCING ACT

Tom Ecker, now of Cedar Rapids, was a student at the University of Iowa in 1955 when this photo was taken. He put together a variety act and appeared at service clubs and meetings. The act helped pay his way through college. (*Submitted by Tom Ecker*)

STEPPING OUT

A photographer from Walkers Drug at 212 Third Ave. SE kept busy in 1955 taking pictures as people walked by. This is Berle Mounts of Cedar Rapids. She bought a copy of this photo and sent it to a relative with the following message on the back. "Hope you like it. I don't." (*Submitted by Teresa Davis, granddaughter of Berle Mounts*)

Leona Kaplan wasn't expecting to have her photo taken by a street photographer in 1955. Her daughter said the photo probably was taken on a Saturday by a photographer for Walkers Drug at 212 Third Ave. SE. She said her mother would visit downtown for the department stores and "dime stores." Her last Saturday stop was always in Czech Village for groceries and meat. The photographer presented a card to each person photographed so they could come in and look at the picture before they purchased it. (*Submitted by Fern Fackler, daughter of Leona Kaplan*)

DELIVERY TIME

William Mikulecky delivered for Dow's Maniti Dairy in northwest Cedar Rapids in 1955. (*Submitted by Karen Millard*)

PARADE

This was the lineup for a Czech Parade on the First Avenue bridge in downtown Cedar Rapids in 1956. Members of the Prairie High School band are in the wagon. Tractor driver is Walter Faltis. (*Submitted by William Faltis*)

Coming home to Cedar

1955

Herald Smith and his wife, Miriam, purchase Cedar Rapids Steel Transportation and set up shop in a refurbished chicken coop they buy for $125.

1963

CRST's expanded intrastate authority allows CRST to transport general commodities and propels the company to $1 million in annual revenue.

1980/81

CRST Inc.'s revenues top $50 million.

Following the passage of the 1980 Motor Carrier Reform Act, which essentially de-regulates the trucking industry, CRST becomes one of the first trucking companies to receive nationwide operating authority.

Rapids for 50 Years.

CRST International, Inc. is formed to integrate all companies under one holding company.

CRST Van Expedited, a CRST International company, moves into its new $5 million headquarters at the site of the former Randall Foods building. CRST International's corporate headquarters is nearby.

CRST International achieves $600 million in annual revenues.

1985   1993   2004

CRST International opens its new corporate headquarters in Cedar Rapids.

THE TRANSPORTATION SOLUTION™

CRST™ 1955 **50** 2005

INTERNATIONAL

IN IT FOR THE LONG HAUL

STUDYING HARD – Georgia Colbert (seated at table) works with a preschool student in 1955 in the first preschool founded by Arc of East Central Iowa. The school was located in the 300 block of E Avenue NW. (*Submitted by Arc*)

HAPPY CAMPERS

Arc campers were headed for a swim at Waubeek Scout Camp in this 1956 photo. (*Submitted by Arc*)

CLIPPING CREW

A class of students poses in front of the Cedar Rapids Barber College at 218 First St. SE. The year was 1956. (*Submitted by Francis Tonns, manager*)

IT'S SPRING

Customers lined up at the Dairy Queen, coats and all, was a sure sign of spring in 1956. This photo was taken March 14, 1956, at the Dairy Queen owned by the Bill Lana family at Third Street and Third Avenue SW. *(Submitted by Bill Lana)*

SERVING THE NEIGHBORHOOD

For 50 years there was a Dlask grocery at 1532 Ellis Blvd. NW. Lumir and Elma Dlask purchased the store for $10,000 in 1948. Ely's Food Shop was at this location before that. This photo was probably taken around 1950. The Dlask's daughter, Karen, bought the store from her parents in 1979. It was closed and torn down in 1998. The 1970s were the busiest time at the store. *(Gazette photo collection)*

WALTZ TIME

The Farm Bureau was the host for a dance at the Armar Ballroom on Nov. 7, 1957. The ballroom, advertised as being "on the boulevard" (First Avenue) between Marion and Cedar Rapids, opened in September 1948 with the Harry James orchestra. It was the largest ballroom in the state with room for 2,500 dancers and 1,500 people seated. It was part of Ce-Mar Acres, which also had an amusement park and a race track. (*Submitted by Robert Zeman*)

PARTY TIME

Mr. and Mrs. E.M. Perkins were among the crowd dancing at the Cedar Rapids Moose Club on New Year's Eve 1957. (*Submitted by Robert Zeman*)

SWING YOUR PARTNER

Betty and Lynn Mineck have been square dancing since 1952 at the ZCBJ Hall at 12th Avenue and Third Street SE. This photo was taken in 1957. Betty Stephensen and Lynn Mineck lived a block away from each other while they were growing up in Cedar Rapids. They later married. (*Submitted by Betty Mineck*)

SURGERY

Dr. John Kanealy (left), urologist, is assisted by nurse Theresa Ockenfels (center) while performing surgery in 1957 at Mercy Hospital in Cedar Rapids (now Mercy Medical Center). At right is Dr. William Kruckenberg, anesthesiologist. (*Mercy Medical Center photo*)

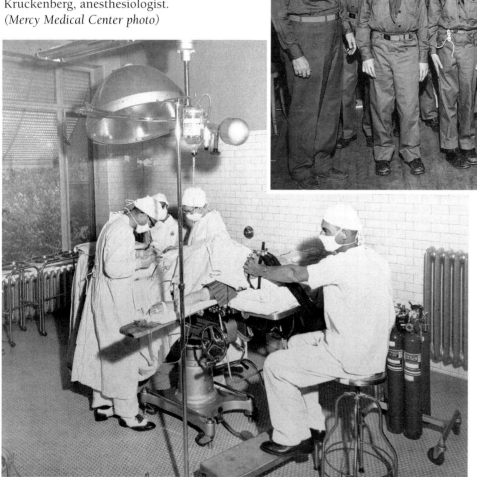

BE PREPARED

VFW Post 788 sponsored Boy Scout Troop 59 in 1957. In first row (from left): Jim Lundstrom, Bobby Close, Dale Gowey, Gary Pyles, Jim Morrow, Charles Hollenhors, unidentified, Doug Hahn. Second row: Merlin Struck, Jim Balsanek, Don Rebeck, unidentified, Art Sallac, Henry Hunter, Don Gillick. Back row: Unidentified, Keith Churchill, Jerry Nixon. (*Submitted by Arc*)

AIMING FOR STARDOM

Members of the Hawkeyes, a vocal music group of University of Iowa students, are shown in a Capitol Studios recording studio in Hollywood in 1957. Members were Dixie Davenport of Anamosa; Don Roeder of Waterloo; Derk Simonson of LaGrange, Ill.; and Jim Williams of Atlantic. They performed for several years and were picked as one of the top new groups by Billboard Magazine but decided to finish college. (*Submitted by Tom Ecker*)

MAMIE'S HERE – Mamie Doud Eisenhower visited Jackson Elementary School on Oct. 17, 1958, while her husband, President Dwight D. Eisenhower, attended the National Corn Picking Contest northeast of Marion. Mamie was 6 months old when she and her family moved to Cedar Rapids in 1896. The family moved 11 years later. Her formal education began at Jackson on Fourth Avenue SE. In the same kindergarten class were Robert Armstrong and Margaret Douglas (Hall). Mamie's father, John Doud, was a department head at the Sinclair packing plant. (*Gazette photo*)

CLIPPER CEDAR RAPIDS – Those words can be seen to the right side of the door at the top of the ramp of this Pan American plane sitting at Gate 4 at the Cedar Rapids airport in 1958. This is believed to be the plane that brought Mamie Doud Eisenhower and others to Cedar Rapids on Oct. 17, 1958. Sutherland Cook, who is in the crowd greeting the plane, recalled when she came. Mrs. Eisenhower was in Cedar Rapids because her husband, President Dwight D. Eisenhower, was visiting the National Corn Picking Contest being held northeast of Marion. She visited Jackson School, which she attended as a child and was honored at a luncheon at the Roosevelt Hotel. Others in the crowd included Robert Armstrong, Russ Landis and Shirley Clark Gilchrist. (*Submitted by Tom Ecker*)

WALKING THE BEAT
The first three Parkettes in Cedar Rapids, Anna Urba, Betty Miller and Carol Upah, are shown in 1958 ready to begin their walking routes downtown. (*Submitted by Robert M.L. Johnson*)

BATTER UP – The Kilborn Photo Paper team was part of the Little Bolt League in 1958. Don Buchheister was coach. League teams, for boys 9 and 10 years old, played games at Noelridge Park in northeast Cedar Rapids. (*Submitted by Don Buchheister*)

HEAVE HO
Cecil Reed and Paul Bonnett saw away as they help clear ground for a neighborhood recreation area in southeast Cedar Rapids in the 1950s. Reed, who owned a floor-care service, was the first Republican of African-American descent elected to the Iowa Legislature in 1966. He helped get Civil Rights legislation passed in the Iowa House. A year later, he was named Iowa employment security commissioner. From that post, he moved on to a series of federal labor department posts. (*African American Historical Museum and Cultural Center of Iowa photo*)

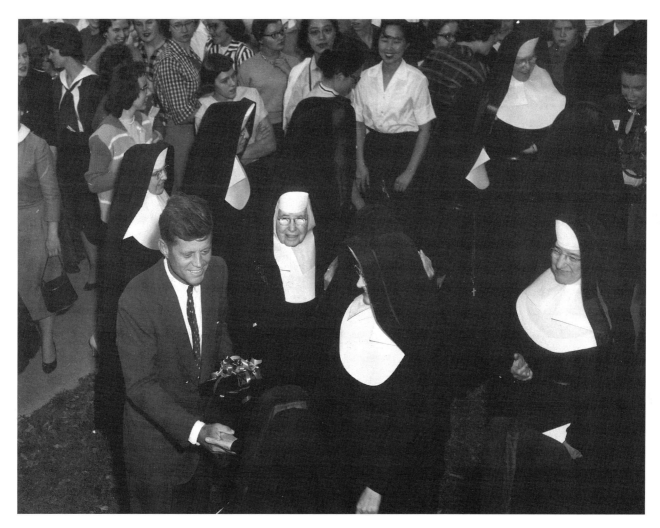

JFK AT MOUNT MERCY – U.S. Sen. John F. Kennedy is shown visiting with nuns at Mount Mercy
College. The picture probably was taken in 1958 when he was in the area to attend the National Corn Picking
Contest northeast of Marion. He was a candidate for the Democratic nomination for president at the time.
President Dwight D. Eisenhower attended the same event. Kennedy spoke from the veranda at McAuley Hall to a
large group that included nuns, students and visitors. Sister Mary Ildephonse presented him with two rosaries; one
for himself and one for his wife, Jackie. (*Mount Mercy College photo*)

FIRE PREVENTION

Members of the 1958 Fire Prevention Bureau stand in front of the old fire station at 427 First St. SE, now the Science Station. From left are Capt. Ellison, Lts. Edsel McMickle, Carter, Anderson, and Robert Barrigar. McMickle later served as fire chief. (*Photos submitted by Robert M.L. Johnson*)

TALKING TIME

Cedar Rapids Safety Commissioner Robert M.L. Johnson held weekly staff meetings at his office in City Hall. From left at this 1958 meeting are Sid Vender and Harry Green of traffic engineering; Police Chief Carl Badger; Fire Chief Jesse Hunter, and Emmett Keough, building official.

PAYING ATTENTION

Mary Jane Donahue and Jimmy Morrow participate in the Arc religious education program at St. Matthew's School in 1958. Teachers were Sister Mary Christopher and Sister Javita. (*Submitted by Arc*)

BATTER UP

Members of the Link Belt Speeder softball team are shown in 1959. Tom Forbes, who submitted the photo, is third from left in the back row. (*Submitted by Tom Forbes*)

OPENING DAY

Mayor Jim Meaghan (at right) threw out the first pitch for the Cedar Rapids Braves opening day in the spring of 1961. Meaghan, League President Vern Holchiedt and Cedar Rapids Kids League President Don Buchheister. (*Submitted by Don Buchheister*)

RIDING HIGH

Free pony rides for children were offered to help get parents to look at model homes in Fair Oaks, a housing development at the corner of F Avenue and 18th Street NW. The year was 1959. Streets in the development all had American Indian names. (*Submitted by Mike Merrifield*)

GAZETTE NEWSROOM

This is the way The Gazette newsroom appeared in the 1950s. In the foreground are Marge Keyser and Ellen Kaupke Howrey, at work in what was then known as the social department. A pneumatic tube system (shown at right) was used to send news copy to the production area. The Gazette has been at 500 Third Ave. S.E. since 1925. *(Gazette photo)*

EASTER OUTFITS

Members of the Hadjis family are shown in front of the Greek Orthodox Church of St. John The Baptist on A Avenue NE on Easter Sunday in 1961. Pictured are (from left) Stavros, Basil, Alex, Bessie and Demetrios. *(Submitted by Demetrios Hadjis)*

Built from the ground up.

(1966)

(1988)

KIRKWOOD
COMMUNITY COLLEGE

Kirkwood
COMMUNITY COLLEGE
Learning for Your Life Time®

THANK YOU

Dora Jane "Dodie" Hamblin and Mrs. Robert (Edna Mae) M.L. Johnson are shown at a 1962 inaugural event for Cedar Rapids Mayor Johnson. Hamblin, a writer for Life magazine, delivered the dinner speech. The event at the Roosevelt Hotel was a thank-you dinner for volunteers in Johnson's first campaign for mayor. A 1941 graduate of Coe College, Hamblin worked for The Gazette as a reporter and assistant society editor until 1944 when she joined the wartime Red Cross. She spent two years in the South Pacific and 18 months in Europe. She joined Life magazine in 1948 in New York City, later working in Paris, London and Chicago before being assigned as chief of the magazine's bureau in Rome. She was there for four years before returning to New York as assistant editor of Life. She left Life in 1970 and returned to Italy to live. She later wrote two books, "Pots and Robbers" and "Buried Cities and Ancient Treasures" about findings of past civilizations in Italy. Hamblin died in 1993.
(Submitted by Robert M.L. Johnson)

CAREFUL NOW

The occasion was a visit from Girl Scouts from Kingston, Jamaica, on July 31, 1966. From left are one of the visitors, Phoebe Smith and Ruby Smith, both of Cedar Rapids, Joleen Zieser of Walker and Vernon Smith of Cedar Rapids. Ruby is the daughter of Phoebe and Vernon Smith. The event was held at the Smith home at 3227 Carlisle St. NE.
(African American Historical Museum and Cultural Center of Iowa photo)

GLAD TO SEE YOU

Former Presidents Harry Truman (left) and Herbert Hoover meet Aug. 10, 1962, in front of the Roosevelt Hotel in downtown Cedar Rapids. That was the starting point for their ride to West Branch for the dedication of the Herbert Hoover Presidential Library-Museum. (*Gazette photo*)

INDEX

Agriculture – 53, 61

Aircraft/airport – 51, 85, 102, 131, 133, 134, 145

Business leaders – 119, 123

Celebrities – 24, 70, 71, 111, 113, 130, 135, 144, 147, 152, 153

Children – 2, 3, 4, 18, 24, 30, 41, 69, 74, 75, 94, 118, 120, 124, 126, 133, 135

Churches/Mosque

    Bethel African Methodist Episcopal – 69

    Joint service involving five churches – 43

    Mosque – 95

    St. Patrick's Catholic – 132

    Salem – 79

    Trinity Methodist Episcopal – 107

    Westminster Presbyterian – 28

Colleges/universities

    Coe – 66, 67

    Mount Mercy – 90, 109, 147

    University of Iowa – 119, 133, 136

Construction – 25, 52, 77, 80, 96

Families

    Banks – 120

    Biederman – 23

    Cargin – 2

    Donnels – 113

    Evans – 47

    Frink – 25

    Frish – 2

    Gallagher – 114

    Geismer – 2

    Hadish – 58

    Hadjis – 126, 150

    Hahn – 59

    Horsky – 3

    Johnson – 4

    Kaplan – 136

    Kula – 74

    Milligan – 8, 61

    Mounts – 136

    Reed – 87, 146

    Rice – 45, 102

    Rodriquez – 126

    Smith – 152

    Stephenson … 8, 102

    Suchomel – 90

    Taylor – 120

    Warren – 31

    Yost – 3

Flood – 88, 89

Fires, firefighters – 13, 50, 55, 60, 76, 81, 104, 148

Government – 78, 80, 146, 148

Homes – 27, 58, 121

Hospitals – 38, 91, 143

Hotels – 34

Landmarks – 13, 19

Manufacturers

    Cedar Rapids Carriage Works – 46

    Century Engineering – 112

    Iowa Manufacturing – 111, 114

    Iowa Steel – 29

INDEX

J.G. Cherry – 30
LaPlant Choate – 100
Perfection Mfg. Co. – 31
Williams & Hunting – 42
Military – 52, 62, 110, 111, 114
Motor vehicles – 23, 35, 38, 40, 48, 55, 56, 60, 68,
    72, 86, 87, 105, 110
Music/dance – 64, 94, 125, 131, 142
Organizations
    Boy Scout Troop 59 – 143
    Criterion Club – 127
    Girl Scouts – 152
    Iowa Consistory, Scottish Rite Masons – 34,
        116, 117
    Iowa Sheet Metal Contractors Assn. – 76
    Knights of Khorassan – 64
    Moose Club Girls Drum and Bugle Corps – 123
    Prince Hall Grand Lodge of Iowa – 128
    33rd Degree Masons – 93
    Women's Relief Corps – 11
    YMCA's World Champion Boys Drum
    and Bugle Corps – 103
Parades – 1, 24, 32, 59, 109, 132, 137
Railroads/streetcars – 8, 26, 45, 49, 50, 82, 83,
    98, 99, 119
Recreation – 16, 17, 18, 22, 32, 33, 40, 47, 57,
    69, 79, 85, 92, 101, 103, 124, 140, 149
Restaurants/bars
    A&W Root Beer – 104
    B Street Bar – 11

Dairy Queen – 141
Harmony Cafeteria – 134
Maid-Rite – 106
Marshall Perkins – 17
Second Ave. Virginia – 45
Retailers/wholesalers
    Blue Valley Creamery – 23
    Cedar Rapids Bottling – 31
    Cedar Rapids Candy Co. – 37
    Colonial Baking – 91
    Cook's Paints – 117
    Dlask Grocery – 141
    Douglas Starch Works – 63
    Dow's Maniti Dairy – 137
    Duster's Grocery – 97
    Frank John's Harness Shop – 84
    Gatto's Grocery – 94
    Ginsberg's – 96
    Hanover Grocery – 87
    Highland Park Grocery – 87
    Hubbard Ice – 30, 44
    Killians Department Store – 49
    Kramer & Son floral – 6
    Lagomarcino-Grupe – 68
    Mineck Groceries – 9
    Moll's Jewelry Store – 27
    Morgan Brothers Bicycle – 108
    Moyer & Darling Bicycles – 16
    National Oats – 61
    Neisner Variety – 118

INDEX

New Store, Kenwood Park – 21

Quaker Oats – 29

Star Pickle Works – 13

Sinclair Packing – 54

Slapnicka music store – 78

Stepanek & Vondracek Hardware – 14

Sterling Grocery – 39

The Fair – 54

Whelihan's Drug Store – 38

William Aossey Sr. – 48

Wilson & Co. – 62

Schools

Arc preschool – 140

Dairydale Elementary – 64

Harrison Elementary – 28

Jefferson Elementary – 3

Johnson Elementary Orchestra – 50, 51

Madison Elementary – 25

McKinley Junior High – 70

Polk Elementary – 41

Rosedale Elementary – 101

Roosevelt High School Band – 105

Shueyville Elementary – 129

St. Berchman's in Marion – 57

St. Patrick's – 93

Washington High School – 21, 92

Services

Barber shop – 14

Cedar Rapids Barber College – 140

Christle hauling – 46

Delivery wagons at Union Station – 53

Gazette – 6, 127, 150

Iowa State Savings Bank – 19

Troy Laundry – 39

New Process Laundry – 63

Republican and Evening Times – 65

Holland Furnace – 72, 73

Lynch Transfer – 73

Skelly Oil Co. – 82

Jarboe Ice – 96

Western Bohemian Fraternal – 112

McCannon's B-Square Service – 115

Street scenes – 35, 40, 43, 68, 90, 100, 107, 115, 122, 129

Theaters – 4, 42, 52, 86, 108

Weddings – 9, 47, 48, 56, 126

INSTITUTION PROFILES

Alliant Energy – 15

CRST – 138, 139

Evergreen Packaging Equipment – 12

Kirkwood Community College – 151

Mercy Medical Center – 20

Quaker Oats – 10

Shuttleworth & Ingersoll – 7

St. Luke's Hospital – Inside Back

Wells Fargo – 5

120 YEARS

A Legacy of Caring

REVEREND
SAMUEL RINGGOLD
PRESIDENT OF THE BOARD
1884-1887

1925

1902

FIGHTING MEN
NEED NURSES
JOIN + TODAY!

So Proudly
We Hail

1942

1935